Ph.D.
Doctor
of
Sciences

Primary 1–3

**Advanced Science
Enrichment Activities**

 Routledge
Taylor & Francis Group

NEW YORK AND LONDON

Ph.D.
Doctor of Sciences

Primary
Summer Enrichment Curriculum

Grade Levels:
1st – 3rd

Length of Time:
80 – 90 hours

First published 2008 by Prufrock Press Inc.

Published in 2021 by Routledge
2 Park Square, Milton Park, Abingdon, Oxon OX14 4RN
605 Third Avenue, New York, NY 10017

Routledge is an imprint of the Taylor & Francis Group, an informa business

Copyright © 2008 Taylor & Francis

ISBN 13: 978-1-59363-253-3 (pbk)

Table of Contents

Activity 1—Pre-Assessment

Instructional Materials
- *25 Fun Adventure Songs* CD or audiotape,
- 1/2 cup of vinegar,
- 1/2 cup of water,
- 2 tablespoons of baking soda,
- 2 hard-boiled eggs,
- 2 paper or plastic cups (with lids if possible), and

Optional:
- 4 copies of **Sentence Strips.**

Preparation
♦ Set up your room like a science laboratory, with science posters, magazines, books, and manipulatives. This will set the stage and pique curiosity. Have the *25 Fun Adventure Songs* CD playing in the background.

♦ Divide students into three lab groups and give them rulers, general art supplies, and writing supplies at each of the three "lab" stations.

♦ Each student should bring in a smock, or "lab coat." Old dress shirts are perfect for this.

♦ Collect three men's ties. The leader in each lab group will wear a tie to designate his or her role as Chief Scientist for the day.

Note
All pages to be used by students or copied by the teacher will be will be shown in bold face type throughout *Ph.D.—Doctor of Sciences*. To locate page numbers for any of these, simply check the Table of Contents located on page 3.

A. As students come into class, have them each assemble a science journal to create a log for the activities they will encounter during their Ph.D. studies. Follow assembly options on **Journal Assembly 1** or **Journal Assembly 2**. Have students put their names on the outside cover. Have several journals already made for late arrivals and to use as samples. Create a mystery box of items that might be encountered during this curriculum or prepare a library of books for students to read after completing their journal entries.

B. Ask students to open their journals to the first page. Have students write the page number (1) at the bottom right corner. (Demonstrate this.) Have students copy the following sentence or have them glue one of the sentences from **Sentence Strips** on to the top of the page.

When I hear the word *science,* it makes me think of …

C. Instruct students to draw and color a picture at the bottom of the page to illustrate their responses.

D. Gather students in a large group to introduce the unit. Wear your white shirt and tie to pretend you are a lab director. Follow the script below or create your own to welcome students.

"Welcome to Ph.D. studies. I am professor _____ and I will be your instructor for the next _____ weeks. I am here to guide you through a series of science activities. Together we will become chemists. (Mix vinegar and baking soda in a small glass container so students can see what happens.) We will get down to business with bugs. (Pretend to swat away a fly or squash a mosquito.) We might get rained on. (Put up an umbrella or hold a book over your head.) We'll examine the life cycle of a star. (Look up or out the window.) We'll find out what keeps our feet on the ground. (Jump up and down.) We'll swim with the whales. (Pretend to swim underwater.) Well, maybe not, but we will learn about animals. (Act like a monkey.) And, we'll explore some things from the past. (Look through a magnifying glass.)

E. Begin preparing **The Eggshell Experiment**. Explain that scientists like to ask questions, such as "What will happen to this egg if I let it sit in a cup of vinegar all night?" Or "What will happen to an egg if I let it sit in a cup of water all night?" Tell them that scientists also like to try to guess what will happen. For example: "I think the egg will triple in size when soaked in water. The egg in the vinegar will simply smell." Explain that such a guess is called a **hypothesis**. Tell students that you will leave the experiment overnight to see what happens.

F. Put the science experiment to the side.

Closure
Ask students to tell you about science experiments they have done on their own. Ask them to share their experiences.

Assessment
At the end of this unit, this activity will be repeated to assess growth.

Instructional Materials
- 1 large sheet of construction paper (any color),
- 50 sheets of lined or unlined paper,
- hole punch, and
- yarn.

Instructions
1. Fold a large sheet of construction paper like a book.

2. Color and glue the journal cover sheet on the front page of the construction paper. (This is the journal cover.)

3. Count 50 pages of lined notebook paper or white computer paper. Place these sheets inside the fold of the large sheet of construction paper. Stack the edges evenly against the fold. Close the notebook.

4. Holding the paper tightly so it doesn't slide, make three hole punches along the bind. Loop each hole with a piece of yarn. Knot and tie in a bow.

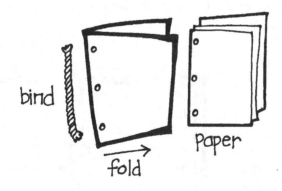

Journal Assembly

Instructional Materials

- 10 large pieces of construction paper per student (assorted colors),
- 50 pieces of lined or unlined paper per student,
- hole punch,
- stapler, and
- yarn.

Instructions

1. Place a piece of construction paper on the table lengthwise. Fold a pocket and staple the sides. Make a pocket for all 8 sciences studied during the unit.

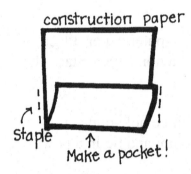

construction paper

Staple

Make a pocket!

2. Add pieces of white paper (lined or unlined) between each science divider to complete the experiments in each lesson.

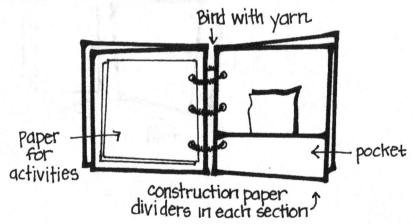

Bird with yarn

paper for activities

pocket

construction paper dividers in each section

3. Punch holes and bind with yarn or string.

When I hear the word *science,* it makes me think of …

When I hear the word *science,* it makes me think of …

When I hear the word *science,* it makes me think of …

When I hear the word *science,* it makes me think of …

When I hear the word *science,* it makes me think of …

When I hear the word *science,* it makes me think of …

The Eggshell Experiment

Instructional Materials
♦ 2 hard-boiled eggs,
♦ 2 plastic cups (lids optional),
♦ ½ cup of water, and
♦ ½ cup of vinegar.

Instructions
1. Hard boil 2 eggs and let them cool.

2. Fill 1 cup half full with water.

3. Fill the other cup half full with vinegar.

4. Place one hard-boiled egg in each cup.

LET THE EGGS SOAK FOR 24 HRS.

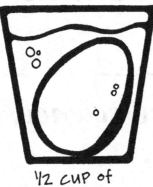

½ CUP of WATER

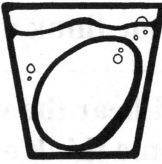

½ CUP of VINEGAR

Activity 2—What Is Science?

Instructional Materials
- science journals;
- *What Is a Scientist?* book, by Barbara Lehn;
- 1 envelope per student;
- 1 copy per student of **Me, Myself, the Scientist;**
- 1 copy per student of **Scientist Skills Cards; and**
- 1 copy per student of **Ph.D. Scavenger Hunt.**

Background Information
Science is the study of nature and the physical world by testing, experimenting, and measuring. The word **science** comes from the Latin word *scientia*, which means knowledge. Science is not just the process of memorizing facts and principles. Science is a way of thinking and acting, and of finding out why things happen.

Preparation
Look over the **Ph.D. Scavenger Hunt** list before making copies. There may be some items you wish to delete or add.

A. Ask students to share what they wrote or drew on their first journal page. Ask the following discussion question: What is science? (Make sure students understand that science is a very broad term that encompasses many fields.)

B. Check on the results of the eggshell experiment. Discuss your hypothesis and conclude what happened. Discard waste.

C. Ask students to tell you what you call people who do science work. Write the word *scientist* on the board, and then have students clap out the syllables. Point out that the letters *sc* make one sound.

D. Continue the discussion by asking what a scientist looks like. Complete the art activity **Me, Myself, the Scientist**. Ask students to display their new looks in class or to store the activity in the journal. Ask a student to collect the journals and put them away for later use.

E. Ask students to brainstorm a list of things scientists do. Supply a basket full of clues or play a simple game of charades to help produce ideas. Lead students to this general answer: *Scientists identify problems or study events to find solutions and explain how things happen.*

F. Share the book *What Is a Scientist?* with the class.

G. After reading the book together, show students the sheet of **Scientist Skills Cards**. Ask students if they have ever been scientists. Ask them if they ever ask questions, learn from their senses, notice details, draw, write, measure, count, sort, test predictions, experiment, think things out, and keep trying even when things get difficult. Tell them that if they answered yes, they are already scientists.

H. Have students color and cut out their own **Scientist Skills Cards**. Place the pictures in an envelope. Label the envelope "Scientist Skills." Make sure students put their names at the top of the envelope. Have students keep the envelopes in their desks or keep them in a basket for later use.

I. Distribute the **PhD Scavenger Hunt** sheets. Divide the list so everyone brings just a few items from home. Students will use these supplies throughout the next few weeks.

EVALUATE!

Closure

Have students tell you again what science is and what scientists do. Create a series of hand movements to help students remember scientists' skills. Record the movements on the board or on chart paper and use them at the beginning of later activities.

Assessment

Assess the Closure activity. Check for understanding.

Ph.D. Scavenger Hunt List

How many of the following items can you find and bring from your house? We will use these items in our Ph.D. experience. Have fun hunting!

old dress shirt (makes a nice lab coat)
newspapers
vinegar
sugar
baking soda
hard-boiled eggs
1 package of dry yeast
letter-size envelopes
empty water bottle
empty 2-liter soda bottle
A-1 Steak Sauce
yarn
pipe cleaners
craft sticks
age-appropriate insect, animal, ocean, whale, and dinosaur reference books
1 empty water bottle
balloon (that fits over top of water bottle)
variety of screw-on plastic caps
2 clumps of steel wool

cooking oil
2 flat containers to hold liquids
lunch size paper bags
grocery size paper bags
sticky notes
string
tape measures
3 egg cartons
straws
marbles
yarn (variety of colors)
newspaper
wire hangers
blue food coloring
baby oil
1 strainer
clean old socks
sponge (to be cut up into small pieces)
shoe box lid or similar size box lid (with sides)
3 plastic cups
6 empty tin cans

Me, Myself, the Scientist

Instructions

1. Color and cut out the figure below.

2. Draw your face on the scientist.

Scientist Skill Cards

asks questions

uses the senses

Writes

Silly about SCIENCE ...have fun!

Notices details

Draws

...Experiments

... tests predictions

Sort

...measures

1 cup

...keeps trying

1..2..3...
counts

... thinks logically

Hmmm?

Activity 3—Lab Groups

Instructional Materials
♦ *What Is a Scientist?* book, by Barbara Lehn;
♦ *25 Fun Adventure Songs* CD or audiotape; and
♦ "It's Called Cooperation" lyrics.

Preparation
Set the CD to play track 25, "It's Called Cooperation."

A. Students will begin today's Ph.D. training with a **sorting** and **classifying** activity from *What Is a Scientist?* Before dividing the class in to three lab groups, assess their understanding of the assignment by playing a game called All Sorts.

B. Select four students to stand at the front of the classroom. Sort students into four groups without telling the class how you sorted them. For example: students wearing shorts and students not wearing shorts, or students with blue eyes and students with brown eyes.

C. Allow time for the class to study the classification activity, then ask how the students are categorized. Call a new set of students to the front and ask a volunteer to do the sorting. Play until the classroom shows a strong understanding of the game. Ask the class what it means to **classify**. (It means to put things into groups according to **characteristics**.) Point out how different individuals were cooperating during the game.

D. Form three lab groups. Explain that the next assignment will be a sorting/classifying assignment similar to the activity just completed. Have each lab group sit in a circle. Then ask each student to remove a shoe and place it in the middle of the circle.

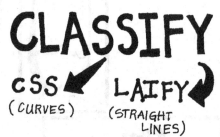

E. Rotate through groups challenging them with probing questions like, "Are any of those called high tops?" to encourage careful observations, measurements, and comparisons. Take note of team cooperation and dynamics. Ask teams to suggest ways the shoes could be sorted or categorized. (Examples include color, length of shoe, width of shoe, pattern on shoe bottom, shoe laces, and fabric.)

F. After groups have had sufficient time, ask students to put their shoes back on and meet in a large group. Ask for a volunteer from each group to tell you how his or her group sorted and categorized their shoes.

G. Mention specific cooperative behavior that you observed, such as, "I really liked the way the whole group listened when Juan was talking." Ask students to tell you why it is important to cooperate and listen when working in a group.

H. Tell students they will be doing many experiments and working in lab groups during Ph.D. Have them help you list four or five rules to keep the groups running smoothly.

I. Have students listen to "It's Called Cooperation" then teach them the chorus.

Closure

Ask students to tell you why it is important for a scientist to listen to other scientists and technicians.

Extensions

A. Teach a basic lesson on linear measurement. Be sure students understand that the end of the ruler must be placed at the beginning of what is to be measured. Have student work in pairs to measure the length and width of their fingers to the nearest centimeter or inch. Create a list of other things they can measure.

B. Have students create category clouds to show how they sorted the shoes in their lab groups.

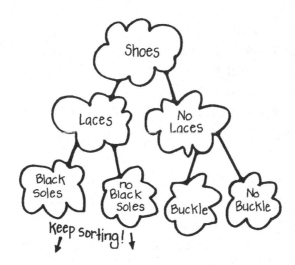

Assessment

Assess the Closure activity. Check for understanding.

It's Called Cooperation Song

Working well with others solving
    problems you will see
Are things that NASA looks for in
    a person who will be
    an astronaut who'll learn and
    share knowledge in a way,
That will help our country learn
    new things each and every day

It's called cooperation—
    I think you will agree
    that if we work together it will just
    become routine
To talk about the problems
    working as a solid team,
    for finding new solutions will
    make everyone succeed!

Now learning is important
    and you must participate
In classes such as math and
    science—really concentrate
For learning quickly is a must
    when new things come your way
And remember the importance of
    the word "cooperate"

(chorus)
Now if you want to be an
    astronaut you'll need to keep,
    your body in good health and
    make sure that you get good sleep.
For exercise and eating right are
    important—don't forget,
    so take good care of yourself—
    and let me just suggest . . .
(chorus)

Activity 4—I Am a Scientist

Instructional Materials
- *What Is a Scientist?* book, by Barbara Lehn;
- 3 copies of **Will It Stop or Will It POP?**;
- 1 cup of warm water;
- 1 package of dry yeast;
- ½ cup of sugar;
- 1 empty water bottle;
- balloon (that fits over top of water bottle);
- 3 copies **Will It Stop of Will It POP? Graph;**
- **What Scientists Like;**
- Journals;
- Scientist Skills Cards from Activity 2;
- timer or stopwatch;
- poster board or butcher paper;
- world map or atlas; and
- globe.

Preparation
Collect supplies for the **Will it Stop or Will it POP?** experiment and set up in a location where it will sit untouched by students. Draw an outline map of the world on a piece of poster board or butcher paper.

A. Introduce the experiment **Will It Stop or Will It POP?** Follow the instructions to begin the experiment, teach about **circumference**, measure, and record information gathered to create the bar graph that will be completed throughout the lesson. This activity will create suspense in the classroom and introduce science and chemistry.

B. Ask students to summarize *What Is a Scientist?* Ask them to line up the Scientist Skills Cards in sequence. Have them ask questions, use senses, notice details, draw, write, measure, count, sort, test predictions, experiment, think logically, keep trying, and have fun.

C. Teach students the song "What Scientists Like." After singing once, have students break into lab groups and create hand or body motions for the song. Allow 10-15 minutes before coming back to the large group to perform. (Allow students to develop their own songs if they wish.)

D. Check the balloon experiment. Gather students to measure the circumference of the balloon and lead students in recording the progress on the bar graph. Ask students before continuing: Will it stop or will it pop?

E. Display the world map. Place a globe on the floor in front of you. Be sure students can see the map and the globe. Write the following title on the map:

Where in the world do scientists come from?

F. Use the following dialogue as an example of what to say to students:

Scientists come from all around the globe. (Spin the globe.) We live here, (point to your location) but you might find a scientist in … (Spin the globe and stop it with your index finger then name the country you're pointing to.) After I find a location on the globe, I'm going to mark it with a sticker on the map. Then I'm going to write the name next to the sticker. I will help you transfer the name, but you have to find the location on the map.

G. Write the names of **countries**, states, and cities on the map. Identify the **continents** and major land areas. Label the continents and bodies of water. (Allow each student a chance to spin the globe. Help students locate different places on the map. If a student spins and touches water, allow another spin.)

H. Check the balloon experiment. Gather students then measure the circumference of the balloon. Lead students in recording the progress on the bar graph. Before continuing, ask students: Will it stop or will it pop?

I. Ask what the information on the graph shows about the balloon. Ask students if their hypotheses were correct. Tell them that the yeast mixed with the sugar in the bottle created a gas in a **chemical reaction** that caused the balloon to inflate.

Closure
Ask students which skills from the Scientist Skills Cards were used to complete the balloon experiment.

Extensions
A. Have students perform more experiments and investigations from *What Is a Scientist?*

B. Ask students how yeast is used. Ask how yeast works in the creation of this product the same way it did in the balloon experiment.

Assessment
Assess the responses to Step I. Make sure students understand and can interpret the graph.

Will It Stop or Will It POP?

Instructional Materials

- 1 cup of warm water,
- 1 package of dry yeast,
- ½ cup of sugar,
- 1 empty water bottle, and
- a balloon (that fits over top of water bottle).

Prepare the Experiment

1. Pour 1 cup of warm water into an empty water bottle.

2. Add 1 package of dry yeast and ½ cup of sugar to the water.

3. Replace the lid, or cover it with a finger and shake.

4. Remove the lid and cover the opening of the bottle with the end of the balloon.

balloon ↘

Student Instructions

1. Look at the balloon covering the bottle. Some ingredients are having a chemical reaction. The chemical reaction is going to have an effect on the balloon. What kind of effect do you think it will have?

2. Hypothesize what will happen to the balloon. Share your answers and record them on the board.

3. You will watch the balloon during the lesson today and record the information you gather on a graph. Watch to see if the balloon is going to get any bigger throughout the lesson.

4. Use a measuring tape to measure the distance around the center of the balloon in centimeters. This is called the circumference. Fill in time passed and allow students to color in the bars on the graph.

5. Measure the circumference of the balloon at 10–15 minute intervals and record it on your graph. You will use your eyes also, but recording information on a graph will help you see what is really happening, and how quickly!

6. After you record the information, set a timer or stop watch for 10–15 minutes. When time is up, measure the circumference again and record the information on the graph.

7. Halfway through the experiment, hypothesize whether the balloon will stop or pop. Write your simple hypotheses (whether or not it will pop) on the space provided on the graph. See what happens!

8. Check your hypothesis at the end of the experiment.

Name_____ Date_____

Will it Stop...or...Will it Pop?

oo (I'm the Title!)

Circumference (centimeters)

26
24
22
20
18
16
14
12
10
8
6
4
2

Start↴

Time
(minutes)

☆Write your HYPOTHESIS here: 2
_____

What Scientists Like

Sing to the tune of "Here We Go Round the Mulberry Bush"

A scientist likes to ask and ask,
A question or two, to keep on track,
A scientist likes to ask and ask,
Ask a lot of questions!

A scientist likes to look and listen,
Touch and taste, and do some sniffin'
A scientist likes to look and listen,
And use five senses!

A scientist likes to notice details,
Big and small, dark or pale,
A scientist likes to notice details,
On everything you see!

A scientist likes to write and draw,
And keep a log of what they saw,
A scientist likes to write and draw,
And keep information!

A scientist likes to measure and count,
Small or short, and all amounts,
A scientist likes to measure and count,
And do all types of math!

A scientist likes to guess and test
Try again, and find what's best,
A scientist likes to guess and test
To find a solution!

A scientist likes to sort and think,
Mix and match, and find a link,
A scientist likes to sort and think,
And learn all you can!

A scientist always has lots of fun,
And share what they find with everyone,
A scientist always has lots of fun,
All day long!

Activity 5—Test Tube Discoveries

Instructional Materials
♦ 3 Test Tube Adventures kits from the Wild Goose Company,
♦ Scientist Skills Cards from Activity 4,
♦ a variety of screw-on plastic lids and caps,
♦ 2-liter soda bottle,
♦ journals, and
♦ **What Scientists Like.**

Preparation
♦ Open the Test Tube Adventures kits and read the adult instructions on pages 1-3. Your students will conduct the "Do-It Tube Discoveries" that start on page 2.
♦ Place four plastic test tubes at each lab station and the pull-out tray in the kit that turns into a test tube holder.
♦ Place three to five varieties of screw-on plastic caps at each station, including one that fits on a plastic soda bottle. That one will fit on the test tube.
♦ Place "The Do-It Tube" card from the kit at each station.
♦ Students can wear their lab coats.

A. Gather students in a circle and review what scientists do by looking at the Scientist Skills Cards from Activity 4. Tell students that they are going to conduct their first independent experiment in their lab groups. Hand out journals.

B. Divide students into three lab groups. Assign one student in each group to be the Chief Scientist. Explain that all students will have this opportunity. Have the Chief Scientist wear the tie for the day.

Note
Assign students to lab groups so the leadership role can rotate. Change groups as needed for classroom management.

C. Show the Chief Scientists (and the class) "The Do-It Tube" card. Tell the Chief Scientists that their groups will use their observation skills to figure out what this tube really is. (Hint: It's not really a test tube for scientists.) Here's what you might say to your Chief Scientists:

> Ask your lab group to open their journals to the next blank page. Instruct them to write the title at the top of the page and the date at the corner. (Demonstrate this on the board.) Ask them some questions to get them thinking like scientists. For example: What is this item? What is it made of? What do you think it is used for? Can it be changed? Have each person in your group share an idea at least once. Then, as a group, predict what you think the tube is used for. Each of you write or draw a prediction of its use in your journals. We'll find out if your predictions are correct at the end of this activity.

D. Challenge students, as part of their observation, to try out some of the caps. Have them draw in their journals what they think the tube is used for. They should write a one-word or one-sentence hypothesis at the bottom of their journal page.

E. Have students work in their groups, then rotate through the groups. Remind students to notice details, ask questions, use their senses, and think. Compliment the Chief Scientists on how well their groups are cooperating. Encourage students to ask questions of the Chief Scientists instead of you during lab time.

F. Return students to the large group, then ask a representative from each group to share what they think the plastic tubes are used for. Explain that the plastic tubes are from a soda-bottle manufacturing plant. They are actually 2-liter soda bottles (display one) before hot air is blown into them to stretch them into the bottle mold. Collect and put away journals.

G. Ask students to compliment a friend who worked well during the lab. Thank the groups for super cooperation.

Closure

Ask students to pull out their Scientist Skills Cards envelopes and place the cards on their desks that show the skills they used in this experiment. Use the picture cards to display as you discuss how each skill was used.

Extension

Sing "What Scientists Like" from Activity 4.

Assessment

Assess the Closure activity. Check for understanding.

Activity 6—Science Specialists

Instructional Materials
♦ 1 copy per student of **Match the Scientist with the Specialty,**
♦ 1 copy per 2 students of **Science in My Hands, and**
♦ 1 copy of **Badges** per student (see Table of Contents).

Background Information
Entomologist—someone who studies insects.
Oceanographer—a scientist who studies the oceans.
Meteorologist—a weather specialist.
Astronomer—a scientist who studies the stars and planets.
Chemist—someone who investigates and researches change using chemicals.
Physicist—a scientist who studies how and why things work.
Zoologist—a person who studies animal life.
Paleontologist—a specialist in plants and animals from long ago.

A. Write the following words on the board: *entomologist, oceanographer, meteorologist, astronomer, chemist, physicist, zoologist,* and *paleontologist.* Have students repeat the words after you several times. Have them clap out the syllables.

B. Tell students that these are just a few of the many fields of science. Ask students to define the words on the board.

C. Use the following dialogue as a model for beginning the exercise:

These are the names of different kinds of scientists. Each studies something different. Let's see if we can guess what they do. Look for clue words to help you. After each guess, I will draw part of a picture that might help you determine what they do. (Have students look for clues in parts of the words, like "ocean" in oceanographer, "zoo" in zoologist, and "meteor" in meteorologist.

Drawing Suggestions
Entomologist—a bug   Oceanographer—a fish
Meteorologist—a rain cloud Astronomer—a shooting star or Saturn
Chemist—bubbling test tubes Physicist—a snowflake, water in a glass, steam from a pot.
Zoologist—an elephant   Paleontologist—a mummy or dinosaur bones

D. Have students discover what these words have in common. Point out the "er" and "ist" endings. Explain that many job titles have these endings. Ask students to list such jobs to prove the point. (teacher, lawyer, painter, artist, pharmacist, novelist, etc.)

Note

Students will probably call out jobs that end with "or" like doctor and "ian" like librarian. Add these to the list then go back and explain that these word endings also indicate a type of job.

E. Tell students that while they are working on Ph.D. they will actually become scientists in the eight fields of study listed on the board. Have them match the words with the pictures on **Match the Scientist with the Specialty**.

F. Have students return to a large group. Review each field of study, then ask students to think about which scientist they would be most interested in learning about.

G. Create a simple "tally mark" graph using the list of scientists. Identify which has the most interest by counting tally marks. This is an opportunity to use sequencing, with a discussion of greatest to least interest.

H. Explain that students will have a chance to earn eight badges, one for each field they will study.

Closure

Teach the song **Science in My Hands**.

Extension

Have students each draw a picture of themselves as the scientist in which they are most interested. They should draw a picture in their journals of what they think they might be doing in that field of study. They should write a word or sentence that describes the scientist's work. Have students write their names at the top of the page as Professor (last name).

Assessment

Assess the accuracy of the answers on **Match the Scientist with the Specialty**.

Match the Science with the Specialty

Entomologist
Meteorologist
Chemist
Oceanographer
Astronomer
Paleontologist
Physicist
Zoologist

Science in My Hands

Sing to the tune of "He's Got the Whole World in His Hands"

I've got the whole world of science,
In my hands.
I've got the whole world of science,
In my hands.
I've got the whole world of science,
In my hands.
I'm earning my Ph.D.!
(Pretend to hold the world up above your head.)

I've got lab coats and bubbles,
In my hands.
I've got lab coats and bubbles,
In my hands.
I've got lab coats and bubbles,
In my hands.
I'm learning my chemistry!
(Pretend to blow bubbles.)

I've got bugs and spiders,
In my hands.
I've got bugs and spiders,
In my hands.
I've got bugs and spiders,
In my hands.
I'm an entomologist!
(Pretend spiders are crawling all over.)

I've got thunderstorms and raindrops,
In my hands.
I've got thunderstorms and raindrops,
In my hands.
I've got thunderstorms and raindrops,
In my hands.
I'm a meteorologist!
(Wiggle your hands down like rain.)

I've got the stars and the planets,
In my hands.
I've got the stars and the planets,
In my hands.
I've got the stars and the planets,
In my hands.
I'm learning my astronomy!
(Point to the sky with alternating hands.)

I've got the oceans and waves,
In my hands.
I've got the oceans and waves,
In my hands.
I've got the oceans and waves,
In my hands.
I'm an oceanographer!
(Make a wave with alternating hands.)

I've got the animal kingdom,
In my hands.
I've got the animal kingdom,
In my hands.
I've got the animal kingdom,
In my hands.
I'm studying zoology!
(Act like your favorite animal.)

I've got dinosaurs and fossils,
In my hands.
I've got dinosaurs and fossils,
In my hands.

I've got dinosaurs and fossils,
In my hands.
I'm a paleontologist!
(Act like your favorite dinosaur.)

I've got machines and sound waves,
In my hands.
I've got machines and sound waves,
In my hands.
I've got machines and sound waves,
In my hands.
I'm studying my physics now!
(Pretend to push and pull.)

I've got the whole world of science,
In my hands.
I've got the whole world of science,
In my hands.
I've got the whole world of science,
In my hands.
I'm earning my Ph.D.!
(Pretend to hold the world up above your head.)

Activity 7—Chemistry, Please

Instructional Materials
- *25 Fun Adventure Songs* CD or audiotape,
- 1 copy per 2 students of **It's Called Chemistry,**
- 1 copy per 2 students of **Raising Rusty,**
- student journals,
- 2 clumps of steel wool,
- oil,
- 2 flat containers to hold liquids,
- 2 craft sticks,
- permanent marker, and

Optional:
- yarn or rope for arms and legs.

Preparation
Set the CD to play track 14, "It's Called Chemistry." Before the activity, read the prompt for the experiment Raising Rusty.

A. Ask students to define **chemistry**. (Chemistry is the study of substances, what they are composed of, and how they react together.)

B. Teach the students the song, "It's Called Chemistry." Explain that H_2O, which is in the lyrics of the song, is the scientific formula for water (2 hydrogen atoms and 1 oxygen atom = a molecule of water).

C. Ask students whether the lyrics helped explain what chemistry is. Have students listen again and list things that teach about chemistry (finding out the cause of a strange disease, mixing dirt and water to make mud, putting a chemical on a stain to make it disappear, heat from your hand melting chocolate, water expanding when frozen). Share other examples of **chemical changes**, such as when metal on a bike left out in the rain gets rusty, or how hot water can turn a powder into gelatin.

D. Follow the prompts to tell the story called **Raising Rusty**.

E. Divide students into three lab groups. Designate new Chief Scientists. Send lab groups to their areas to gather journals while you instruct new Chief Scientists. Follow the instructions on **Raising Rusty**.

F. Clean up, then store completed experiments in a safe place. Gather the class as a large group, and then make a list of predictions. Ask students what they think will happen to Rusty's hair.

G. Ask students to return to their desks and write the title "Raising Rusty" at the top of the next blank page in their journals. They should divide the paper in half by drawing a line down the center from top to bottom. Ask them to draw a picture on the left side of the page showing what they predict Rusty will look like after a good night's sleep.

H. Collect journals and gather students as a group again.

Closure
Listen to the song "It's called Chemistry" again. Ask the class to sing along. Have students write "Chemistry is …" in their journals, and then have them write or draw their responses.

Assessment
Assess the Closure activity. Check for understanding of the word *chemistry*.

It's Called Chemistry

from Twin Sisters Productions

Do you like to investigate?
Do you like to know?
What happens to the puddles
   that splash beneath your toes?

Do you ask a lot of questions?
Like what is H_2O?
Or why does sugar taste so sweet?
Would you like to know?

Chorus
It's called chemistry.
You might grow up to be…
   a chemist who will help us find
   the answers that we need…
   you might investigate
The cause of a strange disease
   and search for cures to help people
Live past one hundred three!

Do you like to play in water
   and mix in a little dirt?
Now how will you get that spot
   off of your brand new shirt?
What happens when you hold
   some chocolate,
   in your little hand?
And why does water when it
   freezes, start to expand?

Chorus

Raising Rusty

Instructional Materials
- 2 clumps of steel wool,
- water,
- oil,
- 2 flat containers to hold liquids,
- 2 craft sticks,
- a permanent marker, and

Optional:
- yarn or rope for arms and legs.

Instructions

1. Make 2 Rusty dolls using steel wool, craft sticks, permanent marker, and optional rope or yarn.

2. Tell the below story, demonstrating as you read.

    I want you all to meet my friend Rusty. (Hold him up.) He lives around the corner from me. I like his family—they're really nice. Rusty is interesting because he likes to sleep in a water bed. That's OK, but this terrible thing happens to Rusty's hair when he sleeps in the water.

    As you can see, Rusty's hair is pretty coarse. His hair is made of steel wool. The problem with Rusty and his water bed occurs during the night when he's sleeping. When his hair, the steel wool, the water, and the oxygen in the air mix together it causes a chemical reaction. So when Rusty wakes up, his mom has quite a hard time getting his hair cleaned out so she can send him off to school.

His mom decided to try to keep the chemical reaction from happening by omitting one of the three factors that caused it. She couldn't get rid of Rusty's hair because he would have nothing to do with her shaving his head! She couldn't take away the water bed because it was the only way he could sleep. So, she decided to block the oxygen from his thick clump of steel hair.

Since Rusty could do this amazing thing that we can't—he can sleep under water—his mom decided to cover the water and Rusty in oil. Since oil and water don't mix, the oil will stay on the top. So she filled the rest of Rusty's bed until his steel wool hair was completely covered. She crossed her fingers and waited till the next morning in hopes of a good hair day. What do you think will happen?

3. Leave Rusty (1) in a container filled with enough water to cover only half of his hair. Follow the same procedure with Rusty (2). Fill the container half full with water then cover the remaining parts of Rusty in oil so that he is completely submerged.

4. Let the experiment sit 24 hours before removing each Rusty from his bed. Rusty (1), whose hair is not protected from the oxygen with oil, should have rust on his hair. Rusty (2) should have a significantly smaller amount of rust on the steel wool. Try to identify what is created during the chemical reaction between oxygen, water, and steel.

5. Talk about places at home or around the area where you have seen rust developing.

6. Record results in student journals.

Activity 8—What's Your Hypothesis?

Instructional Materials
- 3 Test Tube Adventures kits from the Wild Goose Company,
- *25 Fun Adventure Songs* CD or audiotape,
- 3 copies of **Bubbling Colors,**
- highlighter or yellow crayon,
- journals,
- water,

Optional:
- A-1 Steak Sauce, and
- a penny.

Preparation
Set out a test tube holder, three plastic test tubes, three screw-on caps, "Scientists write down or draw… things they learn" card, and 1 package of Tub Tints at each lab station.

A. Complete the Raising Rusty experiment from Activity 7. Hand out journals and have students turn to their prediction page. Wake Rusty up and see what happened. Students use their Scientist Skills Cards to determine the results. Have students draw a picture on the right side of the divided page in their journal. Have them title the section: Results or Conclusion.

B. Tell students they will be chemists again today. Designate a new Chief Scientist for each lab group. Go over the **Bubbling Colors** experiment so students will be able to do the experiment independently.

C. Write the word **hypothesis** on the chalkboard or overhead. Begin the lesson by asking students to sound out and identify the word. Once identified, clap out and mark the syllables using / marks.

D. Tell students that all scientists form hypotheses before performing experiments. A hypothesis is a scientist's educated guess about the results of an experiment. For example, if a scientist wants to experiment with a test tube filled with vinegar and a test tube filled with baking soda, he might ask himself: What will happen if I mix vinegar and baking soda?

E. Tell students that the test tubes will have to be filled ¾ full of water. Draw a test tube on the chalkboard, and then divide it into four equal parts. Invite a student to shade in three of the four parts. Check for understanding of this concept before moving to the next step.

F. Give a **Bubbling Colors** lab sheet to the Chief Scientist in each group and instruct them to begin the experiment after they record their hypotheses in their journals. (You may need to help them write this sentence.) Rotate to each group and offer positive comments on teamwork and cooperation.

G. Gather students in a large group. Do not pour out the colored water.

H. Ask students to show and tell you what they observed. Comment on whether their hypotheses were correct. Explain that an incorrect hypothesis is an important part of science. Stress that there is nothing wrong with **disproving** a hypothesis. That is what scientists do.

I. Tell students they have just observed a chemical reaction between the water and the colored tablet. A chemical reaction is the process that changes one chemical into another. The tablet, made of sodium carbonate, reacted with the water to create **carbon dioxide**.

J. Ask students to tell you how they liked being chemists. Compliment good cooperative team effort and leadership. Be sure all students feel they are having an equal opportunity to participate in the experiments.

Closure

A. Ask students to pull out their Scientist Skills Cards envelopes and select the skills they used in this experiment. Display the cards as you close the lesson and how each skill was used.

B. Have students define *hypothesis*. Then ask them to share whether their hypotheses were correct. Ask students why it doesn't matter whether they were right or wrong.

Extension

Perform a mini-experiment. Ask students what they think will happen if they try to clean a penny with A-1 Steak Sauce. Create a hypothesis and perform the experiment.

Assessment

Assess the Closure activity. Check for understanding of the word *hypothesis*.

Bubbling Colors

1. Fill three plastic test tubes ¾ full of water and place them in the holder.

2. Open the package of Tub Tints. Pick a blue, yellow, and red tablet (it looks purple) out of the package.

3. Take a test tube out of the holder and drop the blue tablet into the water. Screw on the cap then watch what happens. Put the tube back in the holder.

4. Take the second test tube out of the holder and drop the yellow tablet into the water. Screw on the cap and watch what happens. Put the tube back in the holder.

5. Take the last test tube out of the holder and drop the red tablet into the water. Screw on the cap and watch what happens. Put that tube back in the holder.

6. Write the words Bubble Colors in your journal. Then draw a picture of what you saw happen when you dropped the tablets into the water.

Activity 9—The Chemistry of Colors

Instructional Materials:
- 3 Test Tube Adventures kits from The Wild Goose Company,
- student journals,
- water,
- crayons or colored pencils, and
- 3 copies of **Mixing Colors.**

A. Read the following dialogue aloud:

Have you ever wondered just how someone made the color of the shirt you have on today? If it's orange, did someone squeeze an orange to paint your shirt? What about your blue jeans? Someone must have drained a couple blueberries for those. Or how about all those other funny colors that you hear adults calling mustard, periwinkle, sage, or sienna? What in the world is all that? I mean, can't we just stick to the basics? Red, yellow, blue, black, and white. Why is it so difficult for adults? Either way, we'd better get used to it. Let's figure out how they create all these different colors.

B. Divide students into three lab groups. Hand out journals and instruct Chief Scientists how to proceed with today's experiment.

C. Add the "Mix colors with your eyes" card from the kit and a rubber band to each lab station. Read the directions on **Mixing Colors.** Make sure students understand how to "cross" the tubes.

D. Ask students to predict or hypothesize about what will happen in this next experiment when the colors are crossed. Write the educated guesses on the board. Don't forget, there can be more than one!

E. Lab groups begin their experimenting. Rotate through each group and offer positive comments on proper lab procedures.

F. When students have finished recording their observations in their journals, have students gather in a large group. DO NOT pour out the colored water.

G. Ask students the following:
- What did people's eyes look like when they looked through the test tube? (They appeared bigger.)
- Why? (Because light bends as it passes from one kind of material into another: from air into plastic into water into plastic and out again.)
- What makes the colors green, purple, orange? (Light appears to change color as it passes through two tubes at once. This causes your eyes to see new colors.)
- What did you see when you added a third tube?

• Was your hypothesis correct or incorrect?

H. Students return to their lab stations to complete one more experiment with the colored tubes. This will involve twisting off the caps and mixing colors together. Discuss how to keep lab areas clean while mixing colored water. Provide lab groups with paper towels, newspaper, or a pan or dish to place under the tubes as they work.

I. Place a "How many colors can you make?" card at each lab station, a fourth test tube (dry) and cap, and something to catch any drips like a newspaper, or pan, paper towels. Read **Test Tube Mix-Up** to the Chief Scientists and the class.

J. Give the **Test Tube Mix-Up** lab sheet to the Chief Scientist. Instruct each group to start the experiment. Rotate through each group and offer positive comments on proper lab procedures.

K. When students have finished recording their observations in their journals have students clean up their areas then gather in a large group.

Closure
Have students check their hypotheses. Was anyone correct? Ask students to draw color scales in their journals. Have them show what colors they made by mixing red, yellow, and blue. Explain that red, blue, and yellow are the primary colors.

Assessment
Check journals for understanding of color mixing.

Mixing Colors

1. Take turns holding each of the colored test tubes up to your eyes near the light, one tube at a time. Describe what you see.

2. Cross the yellow and blue tubes then look at them near the light. Describe what you see. Make sure everybody has a turn.

3. Combine the red and blue tubes. What do you see? Do the same thing with the red and yellow.

4. Write Mixing Colors in your journal and use crayons to draw what you saw each time.

5. Stretch a rubber band around all three test tubes and see when happens then.

RUBBER BAND

Test Tube Mix-Up

1. Choose two colors you want to mix.

2. Twist off the caps on both tubes. Predict what color you will make before you mix the colors together.

3. Pour about an inch of each of the two colored liquids into the clean, empty test tube. Swirl it around. What color does it make?

4. Record that answer in your journal under Test Tube Mix-Up.

5. Select two more colors to mix. Record what color you get.

6. Select two more colors to mix. Record what color you get.

7. What happens when you add a little of all three colors?

Activity 10 – Let's Get Chemical

Instructional Materials
♦ 3 Test Tube Adventures kits from Wild Goose Company
♦ 3 copies of **Beads of Joy**
♦ 3 copies of **The Blob**
♦ student journals
♦ water

Preparation
Set out a test tube holder, a dry plastic test tube, a screw-on cap, and a package of Styrofoam beads at each lab station.

A. Designate the Chief Scientists for this experiment. Direct other students to return to their lab groups and gather their journals. Go over **Beads of Joy** until you are certain the Chief Scientists will be able to do the experiment independently. Give the **Beads of Joy** lab sheet to each Chief Scientist.

B. Chief Scientists meet with their lab groups and direct group members to turn to the next blank page in their journals. Students should write the title and the date at the top of the page. (Demonstrate this on the board.) The Chief Scientists should explain that the purpose for the next experiment will be to discover what will happen when the Styrofoam beads are shaken in an empty test tube. What will happen to the Styrofoam beads when they are shaken in a test tube filled with water? Students should take turns sharing a hypothesis, then perform the experiment.

C. Ask a member of each group to share an example of teamwork and cooperation that they have seen going during the activity.

D. Ask students to write a word or sentence in their journals that describes the result of the experiment.

E. Ask students to show you and tell you what they observed. Ask the following questions:
♦ Why did the Styrofoam beads stick to the inside of the tube? (When the Styrofoam beads rub against each other, they produce static electricity.)
♦ Why did the Styrofoam beads float to the top of the tube? (Because tiny air bubbles are trapped inside the Styrofoam and make the beads lighter than water.)

F. Tell students that scientists use a lot of math. Ask them why math would be important to a chemist. (measuring chemicals, for example)

G. Draw a large test tube on the board, then use the following dialog to teach a simple fraction lesson:

♦ If I wanted to fill this test tube half way, to what point would I fill it? (Ask for a volunteer to come to the board and draw a line showing ½.)

♦ Now that I've filled it halfway, what if I needed to divide that amount in half? Where would I divide the water? (Have another volunteer draw the line.)

♦ Now, I have all this empty space at the top. What if I decide I want to fill up ½ of the empty space above? Can someone draw a line to show me where that line would be? (Another volunteer draws that line.)

♦ Now look at what we've done here. We've divided our test tube into 4 parts.

♦ (Point to the bottom.)If we filled it to this line, we would have filled 1 part of 4. (Point to the squares.) This is the ¼ marker. (Label the line.)

♦ If I fill the test tube to this marker (point to ½), we will have filled up 2 parts of 4 on the test tube. This is called ½. (Label the line.)

♦ If I were to fill the test tube to the next marker (3/4) we will have filled 3 parts out of 4 parts of the test tube. This is called ¾.(Label the line.)

♦ What would you call it if I were to fill the entire test tube, which means I would fill all 4 parts? (Ask for volunteers, or guide students to the answer.)

H. Explain the next chemistry experiment, **The Blob**. Before beginning, ask students to turn to the next blank page in their journals. Have students write the title and the date at the top of the page. Next, have students divide the paper in half lengthwise.

I. Determine a hypothesis as a group. Have students record what they think will happen when oil and water are mixed on the *top half* of the page. Students can either copy the hypothesis on the board or draw a picture.

J. Give **The Blob** lab sheet to the Chief Scientists and have them start the experiment. Rotate through each group and offer positive comments on proper lab procedures.

K. Have students record their observations on the bottom half of their journal pages, then gather the class in a large group.

L. Ask students to show you and tell you what they observed.

♦ What happened when you poured the cap full of water into the oil? (The water sank to the bottom.)

♦ What happened to the tiny droplets of water in the tube? (They joined together to make one big blob.)

♦ Why do you think the water sank to the bottom? (Water is heavier than oil.)

M. Have groups clean up their lab areas. Discard waste oil and water into a sealable container to discard in the trash. Do not pour the oil down the drain.

Closure

Ask students to think like a chemist for the following problems: If a ship has an accident and spills oil into the sea, what will happen to the oil? (It will float on the water.) What kind of problems could that cause? (The area would become dangerous for birds, fish, and other animals.) What problem would a chemist like to solve in this situation? (how to dissolve or remove the oil from the water safely and quickly, or how to keep ships from leaking oil)

Extensions

A. Review the test tube activity. Have students take turns shading parts of test tubes on the board.

B. Ask students why Styrofoam peanuts always stick to you when you open a package. Ask students if they can discover and share their answers tomorrow.

Assessment

Assess student journal responses.

Beads of Joy

Instructional Materials
- 1 bag of Styrofoam beads
- 1 plastic test tube
- screw-on cap

Instructions

1. Pour the bag of Styrofoam beads into a clean, dry test tube. Screw on the cap.

2. Shake the test tube back and forth for about 15 seconds.

3. What happened? Draw or write your observation.

4. Why do you think that happened?

5. Open the test tube and drop in a Tub Tint of any color.

6. Fill the test tube with water until the Styrofoam beads start to creep over the top, then put on the cap.

7. Turn the test tube over, upside down, end-to-end, or any other way. What happens to the Styrofoam beads? Do they float or sink? Why?

The Blob

Instructional Materials
- cooking oil from Test Tube Adventures kit
- clean plastic test tube
- screw-on cap
- water
- journals

Instructions

1. Open the bottle of cooking oil and carefully pour it into a clean test tube until the tube is three-fourths full.

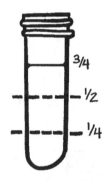

2. Fill a soda bottle cap with water and pour it into the tube.

3. What happens to the oil and water? Draw a picture in your journal.

4. Drop a Tub Tint into the test tube with the oil and water. Watch what happens to the bubbling water on the bottom. Draw a picture in your journal of what is happening.

5. After the bubbling has stopped fill the rest of the tube with oil until it's almost overflowing. Screw the cap on tightly and wipe off any extra oil with a paper towel.

6. Tip the test tube back and forth and watch what happens. Draw a picture in your journal.

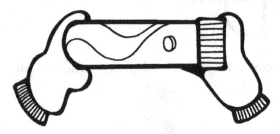

7. What else do you notice?

Activity 11 - Disappearing Peanuts

Instructional Materials
- 3 Test Tube Adventures kits from Wild Goose Company
- 3 copies of **Melting Peanuts**
- student journals
- water

Optional:
- computer with Internet access

Preparation
Set out a test tube holder, two dry plastic test tubes, two screw-on caps, and packing peanuts from the kit at each lab station.

A. Designate today's Chief Scientists. Go over **Melting Peanuts** until you are certain the Chief Scientists will be able to do the experiment independently. Hand out journals. Ask students to turn to the next blank page and write the title and date at the top. Again, have students divide the page in half lengthwise.

B. Ask students to write hypotheses about what will happen to the white packing peanut when it is put in water and what will happen to the green packing peanut when it is put in water. Record these drawings or sentences on the top half of the page.

C. Give the **Melting Peanuts** lab sheet to the Chief Scientists and have them start the experiment. Rotate through each group and offer positive comments on proper lab procedures.

D. Have students record their observations on the bottom half of their journal pages, then gather in a large group.

E. Ask students to share their illustrations or what they observed.
- What happened to the green packing peanut in water? (Nothing because the green packing peanuts are made of a chemical called polystyrene, better known as Styrofoam. It is soft and squishy so people use it to protect breakable things when shipping.)
- What happened to the white packing peanut in water? (It melted because it is made of cornstarch, which is used in cooking and dissolves quickly in water.)

Closure
Ask students why chemists invented cornstarch packing peanuts. (They're better for our environment because they melt away in landfills.)

Extensions

A. Have students brainstorm other things in our environment that chemists could work on to change or improve.

Note

The following Web sites were working and age-appropriate at the time of publication, but McGee-Keiser has no control over any subsequent changes. Please preview all sites before letting students view them.

B. Help students access the following Web site to learn more about the scientific method: http://www.brainpop.com/science/matter/scientificmethod/index.weml

Assessment

Assess student journal responses.

Melting Peanuts

Instructional Materials
- 2 clean plastic test tubes
- packing peanuts
- 2 screw-on caps
- water
- journals

Instructions

1. Fill two clean plastic test tubes half full of water.

2. Squeeze the packing peanuts between your fingers. Does the green peanut feel any different than the white peanut? Write your observations in your journal.

SQUEEZE!

3. Push a green packing peanut into one of the test tubes. Screw on the cap then shake the tube for about 1 minute.

4. Push a white packing peanut into one of the test tubes. Screw on the cap then shake the tube for about 1 minute.

5. Record your observations in your journal.

Activity 12 - An Unusual Child

Instructional Materials
♦ *A Weed Is a Flower* book, by Aliki

Optional:
♦ bag of peanuts
♦ computer with Internet access

Preparation
Check to see if students are allergic to peanuts before using them in the classroom.

A. Ask students which of the following items they think can be made from peanuts: paper, ink, shaving cream, sauces, shampoo, and milk. Have students volunteer information and their reasoning behind their choices. (The answer is, all of them.)

B. Tell students they are going to listen to a story about a famous chemist who helped poor farmers grow better crops. George Washington Carver not only made paper, ink, shaving cream, sauces, shampoo, and milk out of peanuts, he figured out how to make over 300 more products as well.

C. Read *A Weed is a Flower* to the class.

D. After reading, ask the following questions:
♦ Why was it hard for George to get an education? (The schools near him would not accept black students.)
♦ How do you think George got his name? (George Washington was the first president, and George lived on the Carver farm.)
♦ Why did some people call George the Plant Doctor when he was young? (He was a local expert on caring for plants.)
♦ Besides science, what else was George good at? (playing the piano, singing, and painting)
♦ What is the study of **agriculture**? (farming or growing crops)
♦ How could growing the same crop year after year harm the soil? (Different crops use different minerals from the soil. If you only plant the same crop, then the same minerals are used up quickly, which damages soil.)

E. Help students access the following Web site to learn more about George Washington Carver:

www.invent.org/index.asp

Closure

Ask students how George Washington Carver used his knowledge of chemistry to help poor people. (He taught them about crop rotation, as well as the many uses of peanuts, sweet potatoes, and other crops. He also helped them improve their nutrition and showed them that even a weak child born to slaves could make a difference in the world.)

Extensions

A. Read aloud *Louis Pasteur: Young Scientist* by Francene Sabin. Compare and contrast the lives of Carver and Pasteur.

B. Bring a variety of items from home or the store that contain peanuts, peanut oil, etc. Have students identify all the different ways peanuts are used in our daily lives.

C. Use **Edible Peanut Butter Dough** to make a tasty, edible dough.

Assessment

Assess responses to the Closure activity.

Edible Peanut Butter Dough

Instructional Materials
- ¼ cup of peanut butter
- ½ cup of non-fat dry milk
- ½ tablespoon of honey
- plastic sealable bag

Instructions

1. Combine the ingredients in the plastic bag.

2. Seal the bag and knead the mixture together until it turns into dough.

3. Use the dough to make edible creations. What would George Washington Carver make with the dough?

4. Do not reuse or store the dough. Use and eat the same day.

Activity 13 - What's Bugging You?

Instructional Materials
- age-appropriate insect reference books
- *25 Fun Adventure Songs* CD or audiotape
- 1 paper bag per lab group
- 1 die per lab group
- 3 copies of **Bug Body Match**
- 3 copies of **Roll-a-Bug**

Optional:
- *Insects Are My Life* book, by Megan McDonald
- copies of **Veggie Bug**

Preparation
Set the CD or audiotape to play "What Is an Insect?" Make copies of the **Bug Body Match**, cut out the body parts and labels, then put the pieces in a paper bag for each lab group. Get three large pieces of butcher paper per group to assemble their bugs.

Background Information
Insects belong to a group of animals called arthropoda, but not every arthropod is an insect. All insects have the following features: **exoskeleton** (a skeleton on the outside of the body), **invertebrate** (no backbone), three body parts (head, **thorax**, and **abdomen**), two compound eyes (eyes made up of thousands of tiny eyes), two **antennae** or feelers, and six jointed legs. Adult insects may have one pair, two pair, or no pair of wings. Spiders are not true insects because they have two body parts and eight jointed legs.

A. Ask students to imagine they are farmers and have a beautiful crop of corn. Tell them the following: The sun has been shining just enough and the rain has come right on time. Everything is perfect, but there is still something you need to worry about. Can you think of what that is? (harmful insects) Today you will start the study of entomology. Entomologists are scientists who study insects.
That's a big job because there are more insects in the world than any other kind of animal. There are approximately three million species of insects in the world.

B. Tell students that George Washington Carver helped farmers by learning about the insects that help and hurt farming. Ask them the following discussion questions, then use the following dialog as an example of what to say:
- Did you know farmers actually want certain insects in their fields? Some bugs are

necessary for farmers to have a successful crop. Can you name any? (Pause for responses.)

♦ What did you eat for breakfast? (Allow time for responses. Guide students to mention breakfast cereals, etc.)

♦ Well, you can thank an insect for your breakfast. Eighty percent of the crops you eat depend on insect pollination for their fruit and seed production. This means the apple you ate for lunch was actually made with the help of an insect. Luckily for farmers, some scientists specialize in learning about bugs. These scientists work with chemists to make chemical mixtures called pesticides that harm destructive insects like locusts, caterpillars, and beetles, without poisoning the crops or people. Imagine devoting every day of your life to learning about the creepy-crawlies under your porch. These scientists are called **entomologists**.

♦ It's a good thing we have people who are interested in bugs and spiders. There are so many insects that if you weighed all the plants and animals on Earth, it's estimated that ants alone would make up 10 percent of the total weight. Makes you wonder where all these little critters are hiding, doesn't it?

C. Show students a copy the Entomology Badge (see Table of Contents for **Badges** page), which they will be earning during this unit and adding to their diplomas.

D. Explain that before students can study entomology they have to know what an insect is. Have students form three lab groups to discuss what they think insects are and how they can identify them. Select three Chief Scientists and hand each a paper bag containing the puzzle pieces from **Bug Body Match**. Instruct the groups to assemble and label the parts of a bug on a piece of butcher paper or construction paper.

E. Gather students in a large group and have the Chief Scientists share what their groups concluded. Draw an example of a bug on the board and label the parts for review. (Optional: Assemble another bug from **Bug Body Match** as an example.)

F. Share a song about insects. Read the Background Information, then play the song on the CD or audiotape entitled, "What Is an Insect?" Teach the chorus and play the song several more times.

Chorus:
Insects, insects, they lay eggs.
Most insects have six jointed legs.
They help our trees and plants to grow tall.
They're every color, some big, some small.

G. Divide students into groups of four or five to play a game. Have the groups sit in a circle around a die and a playing card. Each student needs a note card or a scrap piece of paper to record scores. Follow the instructions on **Roll-a-Bug** to play.

Closure

Distribute student journals. Ask students to draw and color an imaginary insect. It must include all the basic bug parts discussed in previous activities. Instruct students to create a name and history for the bug. They should include what the insect eats, where it lives, how it sounds, and how it protects itself.

Extensions

A. Ask students how many of them love insects. Record their answers then make a graph. Read aloud *Insects Are My Life* then discuss the main idea and supporting details.

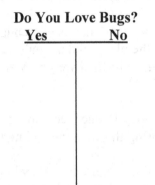

Do You Love Bugs?

Yes	No

B. Build a bug using the **Veggie-Bug** attachment.

C. Share a bug experience with the class. It can be funny or gross.

Assessment

Assess knowledge by checking to see if the students included all of the basic parts of an insect (three body parts, six legs, antennae, and possibly one or two pairs of wings).

Bug Body Match

Instructions
1. Cut out the body parts and labels below, then place them in a paper bag.
2. Have students assemble and label the bug with the correct terms.

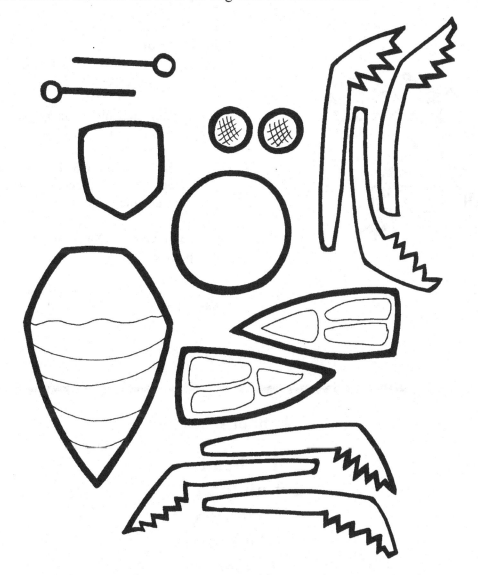

ANTENNAE   THORAX   ABDOMEN

LEGS   WINGS   COMPOUND EYES   HEAD

Roll-a-Bug

Instructional Materials
- 1 die
- pencil

Preparation
Write the number code below on the chalkboard.

Instructions
1. This game may be played with partners or as a group.

2. Take turns rolling the die to gather insect parts to build a bug.

3. You'll have to roll a 5 six times to get all the legs for your insect and a 4 two times for antennae, etc.

4. The first player to assemble a complete bug wins.

5. Play with a partner and compete against another pair of friends.

Number Code

1 = head
2 = abdomen
3 = thorax
4 = antennae
5 = legs
6 = compound eye

Veggie Bug

Instructional Materials
- guide book to insects
- assorted vegetables to make bugs (suggestions include potatoes, squash, bell peppers, cherry tomatoes, corn, green beans, radishes, lettuce, carrots)
- toothpicks
- plastic knives
- edible item that could be used like glue, such as cream cheese
- paper towels or wet wipes
- paper plates

Preparation
Cut, clean, and divide vegetables into obvious body parts for students to use.

Instructions
1. Prepare veggies as desired and lay all the items along a long table that is open on all four sides. Or divide materials so students can work in lab groups.

Veggies!

2. Explain that students will make their own insects out of the food you have set out.

3. Review an insect's body parts. Do not allow students to use knives.

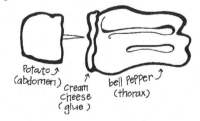

Potato (abdomen)   cream cheese (glue)   bell pepper (thorax)

4. The bugs can be new creations or replicas of real insects.

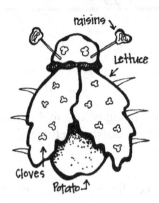

5. Leftover veggies can be used in a pot of vegetable soup.

Activity 14 – Where Are You?

Instructional Materials
- insect research books
- 1 copy per two students of **Walking Stick**
- brown sticks from outdoors
- 3 brown pipe cleaners per student
- 1 insect field guide per lab group
- self-adhesive notes

Optional:
- *Bugs For Lunch* book, by Margery Facklam
- computer with Internet access

Preparation
Find examples of insect camouflage and mimicry in resource books.
Write the following instructions on the board for use in step B.

1. Turn to the next blank page in your student journal.
2. Write the title on the page: Camouflage and Mimicry
3. Divide the paper into four equal squares.
4. Draw and color each bug you chose.
5. Write the name of the bug at the bottom of each square.
6. In the top right corner, identify the insect's defense by writing "M" for mimicry or "C" for camouflage.

Background Information
Insects use **camouflage** and **mimicry** to hide from the **predators** that want to eat them. A camouflaged insect has coloring that matches its background. This makes it difficult for a predator to see it. Ask students if they can think of an insect that uses color for **protection**. Mimicking insects copy a dangerous animal's shape, coloring, sound, and movement. Confused predators then avoid these insects, mistaking them for dangerous creatures. Another form of mimicry is appearing like something other than an insect, such as a leaf or a stick. Use a bug field guide to identify insects with these **characteristics**.

A. Read aloud the Background Information. Ask students if they can think of any bugs that use camouflage to protect themselves, and if they've ever found a bug by accident while looking at a tree or a leaf.

B. Hand out insect field guides to each lab group and have them mark pages with self-adhesive notes identifying two insects that use camouflage and two that use mimicry. Hand out journals while lab groups are looking through the field guides. After the groups mark their bugs, have them follow the instructions on the board for their journal activity.

C. Have students line up to go on a stick hunt. Every student must find a stick to make a stick bug or walking stick. Follow the instructions on **Walking Stick**. Share the following information with the class: Walking sticks look exactly like their name. They have thin bodies but no wings. And don't worry. Even though they look a little strange, they don't hurt people.

D. Display walking sticks. You might want to display them on brown butcher paper or a log to show how they use camouflage. Make sure to tag a leg of each insect with a name so they don't lose their owners.

E. Have students divide into their lab groups and have the Chief Scientists distribute art supplies.

F. Each student will make a paper insect and pick an area in the room where the bug will "hide." Students may use camouflage or mimicry.

G. When all the insects have been made, have students lower their heads on their desks and close their eyes. Then tap students, one at a time, so they can hide the bugs.

H. When every bug has been placed, tell students to open their eyes. Give them three minutes to find as many bugs as they can.

I. Ask the owners of bugs that weren't found to show the class where the insects are hiding.

J. Discuss why some bugs were harder to find. Discuss what would happen to birds and other predators if all bugs were perfectly hidden by nature.

Closure
Ask each student to each tell another student whether he or she thinks camouflage or mimicry is the best protection for insects and spiders.

Assessment
Assess the Closure activity. Make sure there is a clear understanding of the two ways insects and spiders protect themselves.

Extensions
A. Have students read *Bugs for Lunch* to discover who eats bugs.

B. Ask students to make as many words as they can using the letters in the word *entomologist.*

C. Help students access the following Web site to learn more about insects. As always, please preview all sites before letting students view them.
http://bugscope.beckman.uiuc.edu/
http://www.insects.org/index.html

Walking Stick

Materials
- sticks from outside (no longer than a forearm)
- glue
- 3 pipe cleaners per student

Instructions

1. Line up the class and head out on a stick hunt.

2. Have students each find a stick to turn into a bug.

3. After returning to class, give each student three pipe cleaners to use for legs. Demonstrate how to attach the legs.

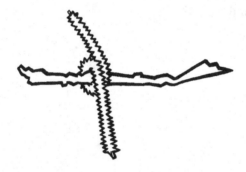

4. Glue on some eyes.

5. Discuss how a walking stick camouflages itself from predators.

Activity 15 – Go Get 'Em!

Instructional Materials
- age-appropriate insect reference books
- string
- yardsticks or tape measures
- plastic test tubes from Test Tube Adventures kits
- tissue or paper towels to stop up the ends of test tubes

Optional:
- copies of **Bug in a Jug**
- 1 large milk carton per lab group
- panty hose (cut the toe so it can cover a milk carton)

Background Information
Some insects, like bees and flies, have wings to fly. Other insects, such as cockroaches, can run very quickly using their legs, all of which are about the same length. Still other insects, like grasshoppers, can jump far distances by **catapulting** their bodies with their long, strong hind legs. Although not all insects have wings, they all have six legs.

A. Ask students how an entomologist might travel to his lab or outdoor location to do his work. (car, plane, boat, train, bike) Use the following dialogue with students: What if we didn't have these convenient means of travel? (We'd have to run or walk.) Insects don't have the luxury of traveling in a car like we do. They get around by their own means. How many ways do insects move around? Let's identify some.

B. Have students brainstorm ways insects travel and list their ideas on the board. Share the Background Information when appropriate.

C. Divide the class into three teams (or their lab groups): the runners, the hoppers, and the fliers. Tell students they are getting ready to open an entomology lab outside to do some collecting and observing.
- Ask the runners to cut a 20-foot length of string.
- Ask the hoppers to cut a 5-foot length of string.
- Ask the fliers to cut six 2-foot lengths of string.

D. Instruct the Chief Scientist from each group to take four plastic test tubes from the test tube discoveries kit to use to hold insects. Each test tube will need a tissue or paper towels to use as a stopper for the top. Students must bring their journals and pencils to record information. Lead the group with their string outside to open the entomology lab.

- The runners create the body of the bug by forming a large circle with their string.

- The hoppers create the head by forming a small circle with their string. They should position the circle so the outside of it touches the outside of the large circle.
- The fliers create the legs by laying the string next to the body. (See diagram.)

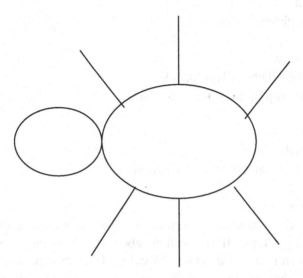

E. Ask everyone to gather inside the body of the big bug entomology lab.

F. Instruct Chief Scientists to gather their test tubes and stand in the head of the bug, which is the *search launching* area. Explain the following rules:

- When I say "Go," each entomologist in the launching area goes out into the school yard and searches for bugs to bring back.
- The entomologist from the runners group searches for insects that run. The entomologist from the hoppers group searches for insects that jump. And the entomologist from the fliers group searches for insects that fly.
- Use your plastic test tubes to catch bugs. Do not hurt or kill the insects. **DO NOT TOUCH the bugs with your hands, and avoid bees, wasps and other stinging insects.** If you question whether a bug is safe to pick up, ask me.
- You'll have three minutes to search. When I say "stop," return to the lab.

G. Say "Go," and watch the search begin.

H. When the entomologists return, they should share their finds with the group. The students observe and draw their catches in their journals.

I. Continue with three new entomologists until all students have had a chance.

J. After students draw them, release each bug in the general area where it was captured. Discuss the following:

- ◆ Do all insects have wings? (no)
- ◆ Do all insects have legs? (yes)
- ◆ How many? (six)
- ◆ Do all insects have three body parts? (yes)
- ◆ Do all the insects travel the same way? (no)

Closure

Have students label in their journals all of the body parts of one of the insects they drew. They should include the head, thorax, abdomen, legs, antennae, compound eyes, and wings.

Extensions

A. Invite a professional entomologist to discuss his or her job and share insect collections.

B. Have students work cooperatively to make a bug house. Gather supplies and follow the instructions on **Bug in a Jug**. Students can use the houses for bug hunts at home or during the week's activities.

Assessment

Assess the Closure activity.

Bug in a Jug

Instructional Materials
♦ empty milk carton, milk jug, or shoe box
♦ scissors
♦ panty hose
♦ twist tie

Preparation
Collect empty containers from home to use for a bug house. Find some old panty hose to cut apart and use as a net around your bug house.

Instructions
1. Clean and dry a container to use for a bug house.

2. Cut out windows on each side of your container.

3. Fill your bug house with grass, sticks, leaves, and a couple drops of water.

4. Cut a leg out of a pair of panty hose. Put the bug house inside the hose like a net to keep the bug in. The twist tie will keep it closed at the top until you are ready to return your bug to the wild.

5. Catch a bug to put in the house.

6. Observe your bug for a day. You might need a flashlight and a magnifying glass.

7. Record your observations in your journal. Draw a picture of the bug and give it a name. What kind of bug is it? What does it do?

8. Return the bug to his real home. Share your story and pictures with the class.

Activity 16 - Great Jumpers

Instructional Materials
- paper clips (1 inch)
- tape measures or rulers
- string

Preparation
Make 1 copy of **Hop to It** for every two students. Find a large area where students can run and jump.

Background Information
Grasshoppers are incredible jumpers. Their long hind legs, which are full of many tiny muscles, catapult these insects great distances. Humans can jump forward a maximum distance of about five times their height, but that's with a running start. From a standstill, the average grasshopper can leap about 20 times its body length. That would be the same as a 4-foot child broad jumping 80 feet.

Grasshoppers come in all shapes and sizes. Some are smaller, some are larger, some are bright green, while others are brown. There are several species of grasshoppers, including long-horned grasshoppers (named for their long antennae), pygmy grasshoppers (the smallest grasshoppers), short-horned grasshoppers (named for their short antennae), and locusts (**migratory** grasshoppers). They can be found worldwide wherever **vegetation** grows. A grasshopper won't bite or sting, so it's OK to try to pick one up.

A. Share the Background Information, then ask students to estimate how far a 1-inch long grasshopper can jump.

B. Divide students into pairs, then give each pair a paper clip representing a 1-inch grasshopper. Ask students to count out 20 inches (20 paper clips) to illustrate how far grasshoppers can jump.

C. As an optional activity, have students search for grasshoppers and measure how far they can jump. Show students how to average the length of the jumps. Handling the insects can help students understand and learn. It may also eliminate fears about bugs. (Grasshoppers can also be purchased from pet stores and sporting goods stores.)

D. Give each student a copy of **Hop to It** Instruct students to measure their height and determine the length they should jump if they were to jump 5, 10, 15, or 20 times their body length. Ask students to see if they can jump that far.

E. Establish a starting line on the ground.

F. Ask students to take a practice jump or two before the one that counts.

G. Have each student run to the starting line and jump as far as he or she can.

H. Have other students mark where the student lands and record the distance from the starting line to the spot where the student landed. If the jumping student falls forward, measure to where his or her heels hit the ground. If the jumping student falls backward, measure to where his or her hands hit the ground.

I. Have each student perform two jumps and record the distance on **Hop to It**. Show students how you calculate the average jump length. (Add the two numbers then divide by the number of jumps, two.) Ask the following questions: How far did you jump? Could you jump five times your body length? Would it be possible to jump 20 times you body length?

Closure
Have students compare **average** jump lengths with their heights. Then explain that they have just proved that relative to its body length a grasshopper can jump much, much farther than a human.

Extensions
A. Teach a lesson showing the difference in inches and centimeters, how many inches in a foot, how many feet in a yard, etc. Ask students to determine which grasshopper is bigger, one that is 6 centimeters or one that is 1-inch long.

B. Instruct students to purchase or catch grasshoppers then test them to see if they can really jump 20 times their body length. Ask students: If a grasshopper can jump 20 times its body length, how big would a grasshopper be that jumps 40 feet? Have them solve for a grasshopper that jumped 80 feet.

C. Gather the class in a circle for a game of Grasshopper Gossip. Whisper something about a grasshopper – a fact or a silly saying – to the person on your right. The person then whispers it to the person on his or her right until the fact makes its way around the circle. See if the statement comes out the same by the time it gets all the way around. Send your gossip around the circle clockwise and counterclockwise.

Assessment
Ask students to explain how to find an average. Give them a simple problem, such as a 2-foot jump and a 4-foot jump, and ask them to figure the average.
(2 + 4 = 6; divide 6 by 2 = 3)

Hop to It

I am _____ tall.
If I were a grasshopper I could jump _____.
Jump #1: I jumped _____.
Jump #2: I jumped _____.

Jump 1 + Jump 2 = _____ (total jump distance)
Total jump distance / 2 = _____ (average jump distance)

If I jumped 5 times my body length I would jump _____.
If I jumped 10 times my body length I would jump_____.
If I jumped 15 times my body length I would jump_____.
If I jumped 20 times my body length I would jump_____.

Did you do it?

I am _____ tall.
If I were a grasshopper I could jump _____.
Jump #1: I jumped _____.
Jump #2: I jumped _____.

Jump 1 + Jump 2 = _____ (total jump distance)
Total jump distance / 2 = _____ (average jump distance)

If I jumped 5 times my body length I would jump _____.
If I jumped 10 times my body length I would jump_____.
If I jumped 15 times my body length I would jump_____.
If I jumped 20 times my body length I would jump_____.
Did you do it?

Activity 17 – Eye Can See You!

Instructional Materials
- 1 egg carton per 6 students
- pipe cleaners
- tape
- straws
- tape

Optional:
- *Charlotte's Web* book, by E. B. White
- computer with Internet access

Preparation
Cut out two adjacent egg cups from the egg carton. Cut a hole about one inch in diameter in the bottom of each cup.

Cutting the straws in advance will save time. (Four or five straws must be cut into four pieces of about the same length.) Make a "frames" pattern for each student on cardstock or cut a pattern out of a manila folder so students can trace the frames themselves.

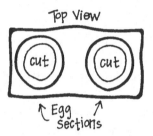

Background Information
Insects have eyes, but they cannot see as clearly as people can. Insects may have simple eyes (fleas), **compound eyes** (dragonflies), or both (grasshoppers). A **simple eye** contains only one lens so the object that the insect sees appears as a single image. A compound eye is made up of many individual lenses. The **image** an insect sees through a compound eye appears as many tiny individual pieces joined together, much like a mosaic. The separate images are collected in the brain and combined to form a single image.

A. Use the following dialogue to explain the benefits of compound eyes.

Have you ever gotten frustrated while trying to catch a housefly? Do you notice that they seem to sense your every move? It's probably because flies, like many other insects, have large compound eyes that detect even the slightest movement. Today you will make a pair of bug eyes so you can imagine what it's like to see through compound eyes.

B. Instruct students, working in pairs, to pick up a pair of "frames" and decorate their bug eyes with antennae and earpieces.

C. Give each student four or five straws. Have them cut the straws into four pieces of about the same length.

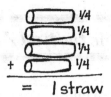

D. Have students bunch seven or eight straw pieces into a round bundle, then have their partners wrap tape around the straws to hold them together.

E. Have students slide the "eyes" into the holes of the frame.

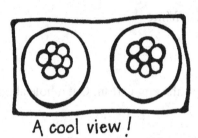

A cool view!

F. Have students wear glasses and make observations in their journals comparing and contrasting their simple eye to a compound eye. Write the following on the board for students to copy into their journals.

With a simple eye I can see _____ like this (draw a picture of what you see).
With a compound eye I can see _____ like this (draw a picture of what you see).

Closure
Ask students to do their best illustrations to give an idea of what it might be like to have a compound eye.

Extensions

A. Experiment with peripheral vision. While one student faces forward, another student stands behind him or her and waves a pencil. The student in front moves only his or her eyes to detect this motion. The student in back slowly moves pencil out to the side. Where can the motion be detected? Do this for both the left and right side.

B. Ask students to name books that have spiders as characters. Introduce the story of *Charlotte's Web*. Share the story between activities or at the end of the day.

C. Help students access the following Web site to learn more about compound eyes. As always, please preview all sites before letting students view them. http://hex.org.uk/insecteyes/

Assessment

Assess the journal entry illustrating the compound eye.

Activity 18 - Feeling Antsy?

Instructional Materials

- *25 Fun Adventure Songs* CD or audiotape
- *One Hundred Hungry Ants* book, by Elinor J. Pinczes
- black construction paper

Preparation

Set the CD or audiotape to play "Ants in My Pants."

Background Information

Some insects, including ants, bees, wasps, and termites, are big on teamwork. They live with others of their own kind in a single nest or home and function as a big family unit. These groups divide up the work so that each member has a job to do. Insects that live like this are called **social insects**. Ants **communicate** by touching antennae.

Every ant in the colony has a job to do, and even though some workers can do more than one job, most only work at one thing. A worker ant cannot be a queen ant. An individual ant cannot decide that it is going to do something different one day. Every ant does what is good for the **community**.

A. Ask students to tell you what they know about how ants live. Share the Background Information.

B. Have students compare and contrast ant colonies and their own families.

C. Read aloud *One Hundred Hungry Ants* to illustrate how ants work as a team.

D. Have students, working in lab groups, tear off 100 small pieces of black construction paper representing 100 ants. Then re-create the story of the *One Hundred Hungry Ants*, first dividing the 100 ants in to two groups of 50, then four groups of 25, etc.

E. Ask students to recall the rhyming words from the story. Write the words on the board then have students read the words back.

F. Listen to the song "Ants in My Pants" and teach students the chorus:

By golly, I believe I'm getting ants in my pants!
Help! Help! Ants are crawling up inside my pants.
It tickles, icky, icky, ickles,
Ants are in my pants.
They're little, itty, bitty, things.
But oh, they made me jump.
And scared me so that they I guess I started to hiccup.

Closure
Discuss the pros and cons of social insects, and of living and working together. Have students list insects that are not social.

Have students finish these sentences in their journals:
I would like to be a social insect because _____.
I would not like to be a social insect because _____.

Extensions
A. Tell students that termite towers are built by family groups working together. When completed, the towers can house thousands – even millions – of termites. The biggest mounds, built by African termites, can be up to 40 feet tall. Have students build a termite tower using directions on **Termite Tower**.

B. Play a game of Hand Antennae to illustrate how ants communicate by touch. Ask students to create a set of hand taps that would tell a blindfolded person to move straight, right, left, or back. Build an obstacle course in the classroom. Divide into teams. Blindfold the first obstacle course player. This person is the ant. The guide will communicate the ant's movements with the touch of a hand or both hands. Teams can create their own hand signals or you can use a standard set for the class. The first team to guide the ant through the course is the winner. Continue playing until everyone has had a turn as the ant and the guide.

C. Observe ants by building an **Ant Extended Stay Suite** using the directions on the page.

Assessment
Assess the Closure activity. Check for understanding of the concept of social insects.

Termite Tower

Instructional Materials
- dirt
- large mixing bowl
- water
- flat base to built mound

Instructions

1. Mix a batch of thick mud for each lab group by pouring the dirt into a bowl and mixing in water until the mixture is thick, like cookie dough.

2. Just like termites, work as a team to begin building your termite mound. Drop blobs of mud onto the flat base to form a pile about 3 inches (7.5 cm) high, and 3-4 inches (7.5-10 cm) wide. Place your mound in a sunny, warm, spot for 30-60 minutes to begin drying.

3. Once your mound base has become dry and hard, the team continues building by adding more blobs of mud on top until you have built up the mound a few more inches. Allow the new "addition" to dry. Continue adding mud until you have a mound that is 7 to 8 inches high. Your mound should become narrower as it gets higher, so that when you are finished, you have a pointed hill of mud.

Note

Real termites use mud mixed with digestive fluids or saliva, which makes the mounds so strong they can withstand damage from weather or intruders. In fact, some termite mounds are built so well, they must be blasted out of the ground with dynamite.

Ant Extended Stay Suite

Instructional Materials
- clear container with lid
- sand, dirt, or a mix
- shovel or spoon
- pencil
- wax paper or a large rock that will fit into the middle of the jar
- small piece of breathable fabric to cover the holes in the lid
- rubber band

Preparation
Ask students to bring a container from home or provide a container for each lab group.
Purchase dirt or sand from a gardening store if there is no area to dig around the school.
Tear wax paper into 2-foot rectangles for students to crumble into a ball.
Use a nail to punch air holes in the lids. (Only the teacher should do this.)
Collect fabric scraps to cover lids.

Instructions
1. Crumble up the wax paper and place it in the jar.

2. Cover the wax paper with soil or sand.

3. After the dirt settles to the bottom, add a couple drops of water so the ants have something to drink.

4. Use a stick to collect ants from an ant pile. Be very careful. Have a friend work with you to pick up one ant at a time. Have your partner push the ant off the stick into the jar using the end of another twig.

5. Collect ants from the same pile or they'll fight.

6. Place a few grains of sugar in the container. Seal the lid and cover it with fabric secured with a rubber band. Don't overfeed the ants or they'll overeat and die.

7. Watch the ants build their new home.

Activity 19 – An Itsy Bitsy Spider

Instructional Materials
- nylon rope or a full ball of yarn
- stakes to place in the ground
- 8 pipe cleaners per student (brown or black cut into equal sizes)
- white paint
- marble
- deep baking pan (large enough to place web at the bottom)

Preparation
Locate an area outside to play the Spider Trap Game. Depending on the skill level of the class, you may want to complete the web before introducing the game. Cut out a web pattern on **Spider Trap Game** from a manila folder for students to trace on black construction paper.

Background Information
Spidersare **arthropods** but are often mistaken for insects. Insects have three body parts and six legs. Spiders, or **arachnids** as they are scientifically called, have a head and thorax that are fused together into one part called a cephalothorax. They also have a large abdomen at the back end. They have eight legs instead of the six that insects have.

The tiny black widow spider has a bad reputation, and it does plenty to deserve it. The female poisons insects. She poisons people. And she eats her mate for dinner. Black widows live all over the world and throughout the United States. She's a shiny black spider, with a red, yellow, or orange design on her abdomen. The design is often in the shape of an **hourglass.**

If you encounter a female black widow, stay away and don't try to catch it. Drop for drop, a black widow's poison is more deadly than rattlesnake **venom**. The bite can greatly harm a person if medical attention isn't found fast. Male black widows are smaller, duller colored, and their venom can hardly stun an insect.

A. Instruct students to open their journals to the next blank page. Ask everyone to draw a picture of a black widow. Share the Background Information with the class.

B. Have students make a female black widow on her web. Set up two stations for working and painting following the instructions on **Black Widow**.

C. After webs have been put together, or if they need some extra time to dry, go outside and play a game using the instructions on **Spider Trap Game**.

D. Discuss why spiders are not insects.

Closure

Hand out Entomology Badges. Allow students time to color and add their badges to their diplomas.

Extensions

A. Encourage students to write a story about a black widow spider that tried to improve her image.

B. Have students follow the instructions on **Roller-Webs**.

Assessment

Have students draw a spider and an insect side by side in their journals. Have students label the differences between the two, then circle the drawing that illustrates a true insect.

Black Widow

Instructional Materials
- construction paper
- scissors
- glue or tape
- crayons or markers
- 4 pipe cleaners per student

Preparation
Prepare spider bodies in advance of having students cut their own.

Instructions
1. Trace two circles on a piece of construction paper. Trace a head (smaller circle) and an abdomen (larger circle). Cut out and glue the pieces together to make your spider.

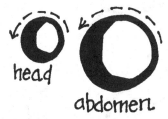

2. Trace and cut an hourglass out of orange, red, or yellow construction paper. Glue the hourglass to the abdomen of your spider. Make some eyes using white paper and glue them on the head of your spider.

3. Tape four pipe cleaners to the back of the spider. Make the legs as even as possible on both sides.

4. Bend the legs in the middle so that two of the legs point toward the head and the other two point back toward the abdomen.

5. Glue your spider on the web you painted. Beware of the black widow!

Web Pattern

97

Spider Trap Game

Instructional Materials
♦ yarn
♦ stakes or wooden skewers from the grocery store

Preparation
Prepare the web outdoors before the game. Or, depending on the ability of the class, have volunteers create the weaves in the web by tying knots and intertwining the string.

Instructions
1. Find a 10-foot by 10-foot area outside. Mark the square using stakes or wooden skewers, five on each side of the square. Take a full ball of yarn and tie the end of the string to one of the stakes. Complete the square by looping the yarn around each of the stakes. Some may need to be secured with knots.

2. Weave a web between the stakes. Leave some spaces at least 1 foot so there will be some spaces to maneuver your feet. Knot off the end of the yarn and make sure all the stakes are secure before the beginning of the game. Tie bells or noise makers to parts of the yarn so you can hear when a "bug" gets caught in the web.

3. Tell the students they are bugs on a mission. Challenge them to get to the other side of the web without disturbing the spider and becoming its meal. Bugs that ring the bell get served for lunch and have to sit on the sidelines and wait for the other bugs to pass.

4. Make it even harder by setting a time limit. The spider is full when there is only one bug left – the winner.

Roller-Webs

Instructional Materials
♦ black construction paper
♦ white paint
♦ marble
♦ deep pie pan
♦ web pattern
♦ tongs
♦ white crayon

Preparation
Prepare a container to hold the paint and the marble. Make sure the tongs can get the marble out of the container. Cutting webs in advance could save time. Cover the area with newspaper or an old sheet. Locate an area for drying.

Instructions
1. Cut out a web from black construction paper. Use a white crayon to trace the web and cut it out. Write your name on the back with the crayon before painting.

2. Place the web inside the cooking tray or pan (name side down).

3. Using the tongs, remove the marble from the paint container.

4. Put the marble in the pan and roll it around the pan. Your web should start to come alive as you roll. Add more paint to the marble as needed.

5. Return the marble to the paint container. Put your web in a safe place to dry.

6. Wipe excess paint from the pan.

Activity 20—Weather Folklore

Instructional Materials
♦ 2 weather thermometers,
♦ 1 Meteorology Badge per student,
♦ construction paper (large manila and red).

Preparation
Prepare the classroom weather chart (See **Weather Chart Sample**) for the week and display it in a group area of classroom. Make patterns from **Thermo-Pat** on cardstock or a file folder. Make copies of the Meteorology Badge. If desired, buy crickets from a pet supply store.

Background Information
Predicting the weather has been a human passion for ages. Farmers wanted to know what kind of a season was coming. Would there be enough rain or would there be drought? Would the winter be cold or mild? How could they tell if a violent storm was coming? Before TV, weather reports, or Doppler radar, people relied on natural signs to help them predict the weather.

The study of weather began many centuries ago with a scientist named Aristotle. Aristotle lived in ancient Greece about 340 B.C. He studied the weather and the climate. Back then, anything that fell from the sky (rain or snow) or anything that was in the sky (like clouds) was called a meteor. The term meteor comes from the Greek word *meteoros*, which means "high in the sky." This is how meteorology got its name.

Meteorology is the study of Earth's atmosphere and weather. Meteorologists specialize in studying weather and its changes. They study the air composition, temperature, pressure, wind speed, direction, precipitation, and humidity. They also study clouds, weather systems, seasons, hurricanes, tornadoes, and even rainbows. All of this is controlled by the sun and the tilt of the Earth on its axis. Meteorologists watch for anything falling from the sky or floating around in it. Thanks to modern science, meteorologists don't just have to rely on their senses anymore. From wind vanes to space satellites, the weather is watched with hundreds of instruments around the globe.

A. Ask students what they think entomology, the study of insects, might have to do with **meteorology**, the science of **forecasting** or **predicting** weather. (Share the Background Information.) Many people believe insects can be good indicators of upcoming weather. Entomologists have found that some of the old sayings about insects and weather are accurate. Some of those sayings or beliefs are listed below.

♦ Locusts sing when the air is hot and dry.
♦ If spiders weave their webs before noon, the weather will be fair.
♦ Ants and cockroaches are busier before a storm.
♦ Crickets sing loudly before violent storms.
♦ If wasps build their nests high, a severe winter is on its way.
♦ When ants travel in a straight line, expect rain; when they scatter, expect fair weather.
♦ Flies bite more before a rain.
♦ Bees will not swarm before a storm.

B. Explain that entomologists and meteorologists agree that crickets can tell temperatures. Play the following game to demonstrate.

Have students sit in a large circle. One student acts like the cricket. The cricket hides in the room and chirps. The rest of the students count the chirps within 15 seconds. Write the number of chirps on the board, then add 37 to that number. That usually turns out to be the temperature of the ground where the cricket is sitting. (number of chirps + 37 = temperature)

C. Tell students that unless they can carry a cricket around, they will have to learn how to read a thermometer. Set a thermometer outside in the sun and another outside in the shade. Return to read both in a few minutes. Have students work as partners to make a thermometer using **Thermometer**.

D. Go outside and find out what the temperature is in the sun and in the shade. Have students show the temperatures of both areas on their thermometers. Discuss why there would be such a difference between the two areas and why it might be important to know the difference of the temperatures.

E. Record the temperature in the shade on the class weather chart in the front of the classroom. Complete the chart, filling in other weather characteristics that students have observed outside.

F. Share the Meteorology Badge with the class. Allow students to start coloring the badges, and then return them to the diploma binder for safekeeping. Allow students to color their badges when they have spare time between activities.

Closure
Have students read a thermometer in the room. Instruct them to adjust the temperature on their thermometers to read the same.

Extensions

A. Purchase crickets from a pet supply store. Send a cricket home with everyone to keep, or prepare a classroom terrarium. If sending crickets home, tell students to create a little terrarium in a jar and to listen to the cricket predict the temperature. Tell students to give the cricket food and water and release it as soon as possible.

B. Remind students to watch tomorrow's weather forecast.

C. Explain the difference between Fahrenheit and Celsius.

Fahrenheit
Freezing point is 32 degrees.
Boiling point is 212 degrees.

Celsius
Freezing point is 0 degrees.
Boiling point is 100 degrees.

Assessment

Ask students to record chosen temperatures on their thermometers, then assess understanding.

Thermometer

Instructional Materials
♦ construction paper (plain and red),
♦ rulers,
♦ scissors,
♦ pencils,
♦ tape, and
♦ markers.

Instructions

1. Fold one large piece of construction paper in half the long way so it looks like a hot dog bun. Cut the paper along the fold. Give the other half of the paper to your partner.

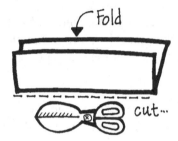

2. Trace a thermometer pattern in the center of one side of the construction paper.

3. Cut out the thermometer without cutting into the side of the paper. Follow the teacher's instructions or ask for assistance to get started.

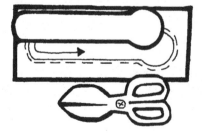

4. Number marks are needed along the side of the thermometer to measure temperature. Usually the numbers are marked directly on the thermometer. We're going to make the marks off to the left side of ours. Using a ruler, make 12 even dashes along the left side of the cutout thermometer starting at the bottom up to the top.

5. Write the number –20 next to the bottom dash. On the next dash up write the number –10. On the next dash up write the number 0. On the next dash up write the number 10. On the next dash up write the number 20. Continue counting by 10s and writing the numbers next to the dashes until each dash has a number next to it.

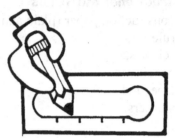

6. Add the small lines between the dashes. There should be four lines between each dash. Practice counting by 2s (in degrees Fahrenheit).

7. Trace the pattern labeled "Temp Reading" on a piece of red construction paper. Cut it out. Turn your thermometer over and place the pattern (handle at the top) on the back of the open part of the thermometer. The top of the red paper should match the mark that says –20 on the other side.

8. Trace and cut the pattern labeled "Backing" on a piece of scrap construction paper. Place the backing over the red construction paper. Secure the backing so that the red construction paper stays marked at –20. The handles of the red construction paper should hook over the tape of the backing to keep it from falling through.

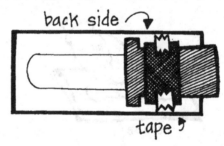

9. The red construction paper should be adjustable, moving up and down, to show a temperature in your thermometer on the front.

10. Write your name at the top of your thermometer. Recycle extra scraps.

Thermo-Pat

(Thermometer patterns)

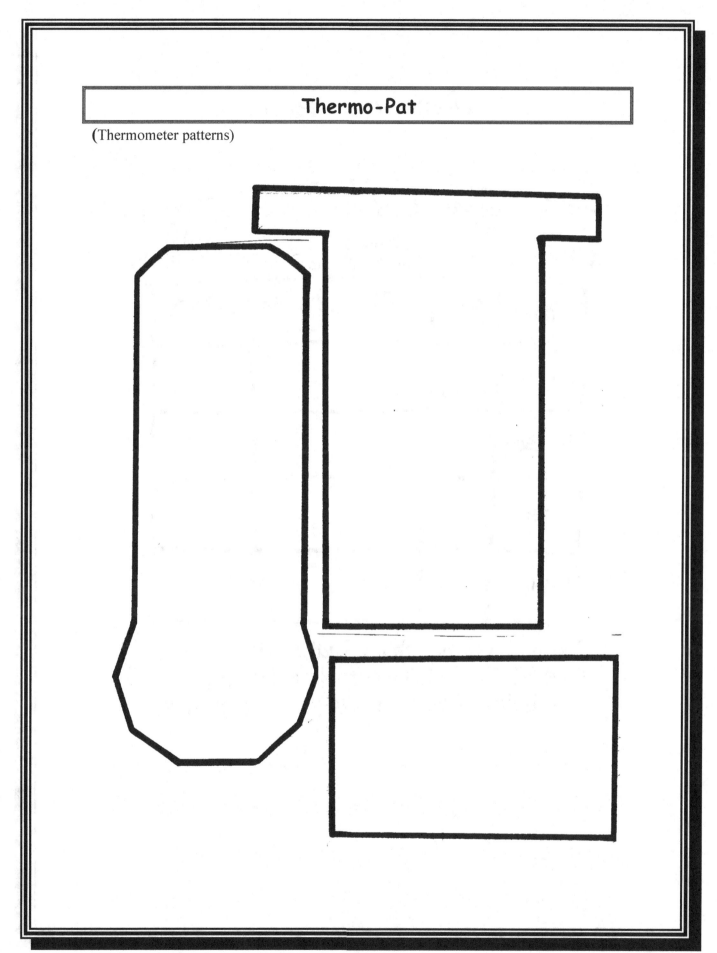

Weather Chart Sample

Make a weather chart that works for you!
Have students help complete the chart
each day. Practice being a Meteorologist!

Instructional Materials

♦ 25 *Fun Adventure Songs* CD or audiotape;
♦ *Cloudy With a Chance of Meatballs* book, by Judi Barrett;
♦ class weather chart;
♦ construction paper (red, green, light green, blue, white, and yellow);
♦ yarn (red and blue);
♦ student journals; and

Optional:

♦ recorded weather report from a local newspaper, forecaster, or other source.

Preparation

Set the CD or audiotape to play "The Weather's Always Changing." Make three copies of **My Diner**.

Background Information

Creating a weekly weather forecast involves the work of thousands of observers and meteorologists around the world. Computers, satellites orbiting the Earth, thermometers, rain gauges, and experience all help meteorologists make predictions.

Large air masses move across the globe in all directions. They can be cold or warm, dry or moist. When two air masses come together, the line between them is called a **front**. Along the front there are usually clouds and thunderstorms. Watch outside the next time you hear the forecaster say a front is moving in. You might experience wind and a change in temperature as the front passes through. Rain and clouds may follow. Movement of these air masses around the globe keeps our weather ever changing.

A. Complete the class weather chart for the day. Compare the current weather to yesterday's predictions. Remind the class that meteorologists can only predict the weather—they won't always be right.

B. Tell students that real meteorologists don't rely on weather **folklore** to predict the weather. They rely on science. Sing "The Weather's Always Changing" to learn more about how meteorologists predict weather. Have students listen for "weather words."

Chorus

From fair skies, to sunshine,
with humid air to breathe,
to cloudy skies, to drizzle,
with thunder and lightning,
The weather's always changing—
it doesn't stay the same
For although we have sunny skies,
tomorrow it could rain.

C. Write the following weather words on the board and see if students can find them.

spicy	thunderbird	heather
mildew	scold	clearly
window	Sunday	Hailo

D. Add more words to your list.

E. Read aloud *Cloudy with a Chance of Meatballs*.

F. Have students break into lab groups to prepare a menu for the restaurant in a tri-fold display. Assign new Chief Scientists to guide the activity. Demonstrate to the Chief Scientists options for creating a tri-fold menu with a large sheet of manila paper. Suggest that Chief Scientists designate menu days to individuals or partners within each group. Ask that the meals be well-balanced. Discuss well-balanced meals with the class before dismissing them to lab groups. Instruct Chief Scientists to follow the instructions on **My Diner**. Have students prepare a menu for their diner in the town of Chewandswallow. Plan the rest of the week after listening to the latest weather forecast. Have teams provide simple illustrations to make their menus more attractive.

G. Have students lay out their Scientist Skills Cards and choose the ones that a meteorologist might use. Encourage students to cite an example of how each skill is used. Discuss these ideas with the group.

H. Tell students that watching the weather can be like reading a map. Each weather change has its own symbol. As they watch the weather on the news they will become more familiar with the colors and symbols. (Share the Background Information.)

I. Write the following symbols on the board:

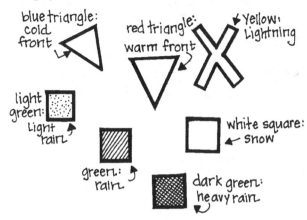

J. Instruct students to follow the directions on **Weather Systems** to make a necklace showing what the weather front is bringing them.

K. Ask students to take turns identifying one another's weather systems. Have them determine what kind of front each person is.

L. Have students study the weather outside, and then make a forecast for the next day. Have each student record his or her prediction on the weather chart.

Closure

A. Have students draw in their journals how the weather changes when a cold front comes in.

B. Ask students to list all the things that help a meteorologist forecast weather.

Extensions

A. Remind students to watch the news for tomorrow's weather forecast.

B. Simulate a thunderstorm by making sounds, then have students repeat the sounds. Start by rubbing your hands together, then patting (not clapping) hands, then snapping, getting progressively louder, then clapping loudly, then stomping and clapping. Slow the storm down by going back through the actions. You may record the "storm" so students can hear how they sounded.

Assessment

Assess understanding through student illustrations of weather fronts.

My Diner

Instructional Materials
- 1 large piece of construction paper (any color),
- white paper,
- pencil,
- scissors, and
- glue.

Instructions

1. Create a tri-fold menu display following the teacher's instructions.

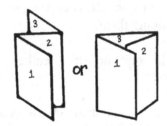

2. Decide on a name for your restaurant. The name will be on the cover of your menu. Select a person to design the cover for your menu.

3. Create a 7-day menu for your diner. Assign each person (or partners) a day of the week. Ask them to cut a piece of white paper that will fit onto one of the flaps of the menu.

4. Each day should include a full-course meal with illustrations that will be glued, in order, onto the tri-fold menu.

5. If you have time, add a dessert menu or other extras to make it fun. Present your menu to the class.

Weather Systems

Instructional Materials
- red yarn;
- blue yarn; and
- construction paper (red, blue, white, yellow, green in 3 shades).

Instructions

1. Study the weather symbols on the board. Do you remember the meteorologist showing you these signs on TV?

2. Turn into your own weather front. Decide if you want to be a cold front or a warm front. Cut a piece of string to make a necklace in the color that matches the front of your choice. Make sure it is long enough to fit around your neck when it is tied together.

3. Cut out blue diamonds for a cold front and red diamonds for a warm front. Fold the diamonds onto the necklace and attach with a piece of tape or glue.

4. Decide what your weather system is bringing in with it. Draw and cut out the symbols on the appropriate color of construction paper. Attach the symbols to your necklace.

5. Wear your weather front. Ask a friend if he or she can guess what weather you're bringing with you.

Activity 22—The Water Cycle

Instructional Materials

- 5 heavy-duty pipe cleaners per student (4 white, 1 blue);
- 1 sheet of light blue tissue paper per student;
- yarn;

Optional:

- ice;
- hot tap water;
- metal cake pan; and
- a wide-mouth glass jar.

Preparation

Prepare ice cubes before class. Locate an area large enough to play Let's Precipitate. Locate an area tall enough to measure 6-feet-7-inches in height. Locate a step stool or chair (for your use only).

Background Information

Every day when the sun comes out it heats the surface of the Earth, beginning a process called evaporation. Puddles, lakes, oceans, even the dew on plants, evaporate. Evaporation is the process of a liquid changing into a gas. When heated by the sun, water breaks down into tiny molecules that float into the air. We call this gas water vapor. The water vapor rises to the cooler air above. As it cools, the water vapor collects together around other particles floating in the air. These particles can be specs of dust, salt, or even small bugs. This collection of water molecules forms a cloud in a process called condensation. As the water vapor continues to condense, the cloud gets larger and heavier. The water vapor molecules bond together until they are too heavy to remain in the cloud and fall back to the ground in the form of rain. This is called precipitation. Then the cycle begins again.

There are two kinds of raindrops. They're not really different when they get to the ground. Where they differ is how they collect the water on the way down. One droplet is called the "lawnmower." This droplet takes down everything in front of it, just like a lawnmower does. As it falls through the cloud, it collects other water molecules, getting larger as it falls.

The second kind of droplet is called a "train car droplet." Think of a train and how it is put together. First you have the engine, which in this case would be the droplet that got too heavy and began to fall back to the ground. Cars are hooked up behind the engine.

Similarly, as the train car droplet falls through a cloud, water molecules attach from behind.

A. Have students complete the weather chart for the day. Compare the current weather to yesterday's predictions.

B. Instruct students to make a hanging mobile illustrating the water cycle. (Share the Background Information.) Each student will need four white pipe cleaners to begin with. Follow the instructions on **Water Cycle**.

C. Play a game using **Let's Precipitate**. Share the Background Information about raindrops.

D. Have students return to group and share the following dialogue with the class: Most of our rainwater comes from the oceans. What is the ocean nearest you called? Imagine that every year 79 inches of that ocean **evaporated**. How tall is that? Use a ruler and masking tape to mark the height on the wall of your classroom. (Mark off 12 inches at a time to count by feet for the next part.)

E. Convert the depth to feet to make a comparison. (6 feet, 7 inches) Tell students the following: Have you ever swam in the deep end of a pool? Some deep ends are 6 feet or deeper. This can give you an idea of the depth that evaporates from the surface of the oceans. Especially considering 75 percent of the Earth is covered by oceans.

F. Ask students whether the oceans lose water. Then explain that they do, but their supply is replenished by rainstorms at sea and runoff from the land.

G. Have students use their Scientist Skills Cards envelopes to identify the skills that they used to perform the experiment. Have students cite an example of how each skill is used. Discuss these ideas with the group. Tell students how to make their own cloud on a cold day by exhaling into the cold air. Explain that when you see your breath, it's because water molecules are collecting together as they cool.

Closure
Ask students how the experiment they just completed relates to the water cycle.

Extensions

A. Ask this challenge question: If there is so much water vapor in the air, why do we have to drink water? Don't we get water every time we inhale?

Answer: The air around us contains different amounts of water vapor. Meteorologists measure the vapor in the air and call it humidity. Near an ocean or a lake on a hot day, the humidity might be very high. If you go to a desert where there is little water, the humidity will be very low. Even though we're breathing it in, especially with humid air, it's still not enough to sustain the human body.

B. Have students design a rain gauge to collect and measure water on a rainy day.

Optional:
C. Have students go to their lab groups, select a Chief Scientist, then complete the experiment on **Indoor Clouds**.

Assessment

Have students draw and label the water cycle in their journals.

Water Cycle

Instructional Materials
- large pipe cleaners (4 white and 1 light blue);
- 1 sheet of light blue tissue paper per student;
- crayons;
- glue;
- scissors;
- yarn; and
- masking tape.

Instructions

1. Connect the ends of the four large white pipe cleaners by twisting them together. Bend the pipe cleaners until they make a circle.

2. Wrap the blue tissue paper around the base of the white circle. Crumple it to make it look like water in the ocean. Secure it lightly to the bottom with tape.

3. Attach the blue pipe cleaner to the left side of the circle just above the water.

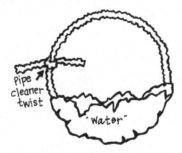

4. Color and cut the patterns on **Water Cycle Patterns**.

5. Tape the water molecules to the blue pipe cleaner.

6. Tape the sun and the cloud to the top of the white circle.

7. Attach the raindrops with blue yarn and hang them from the right side so they look like they're falling into the water.

8. Display the water cycle in the classroom or hang it from the ceiling with yarn.

Water Cycle Patterns

Instructions
Color and cut out each piece of the water cycle.

Let's Precipitate

Instructional Materials
♦ masking tape or cones.

Instructions
1. Divide or mark a square, outside or inside, that is 15 feet by 15 feet. You may want to make the square larger, depending on the number of students.

2. Ask for two volunteers. One will be a lawnmower water droplet. The other will be a train car droplet. The rest of the class will be the water vapor moving around the "cloud" or the square boundary.

3. Ask the water vapor to scatter around the inside of the square for a count of 10. When "10" is called, players must freeze in place with their arms out.

4. The object of each droplet is to collect water vapor particles while moving through the cloud. A lawnmower droplet must collect water vapor he or she runs into face on. The lawnmower droplet holds his or her arms out in front in a "V" shape. The lawnmower looks for the path through the cloud where they think he or she will gather the most water vapor. The collected water vapor must move with the lawnmower, their arms open in the same manner, collecting more particles as they move.

5. Count how many water vapor molecules the lawnmower droplet collected.

6. Return water vapor to the cloud and have them scatter for a count of 10.

7. The train car droplet moves through the cloud with arms out behind him or her in a "V." Water molecules hit by the train car's arms connect to the back of the droplet and open their arms in the same manner. Tell the train car to look for the path through the cloud where he or she can collect the most water vapor.

8. Count how many water vapor molecules the train car droplet collected.

9. Let someone else have a turn.

Indoor Clouds

Instructional Materials
- metal cake or sheet pan,
- hot tap water,
- ice cubes, and
- a large glass jar.

Instructions

1. Fill a metal cake pan with ice. Wait a few minutes until the pan gets cold.

2. Pour 2–3 inches of hot tap water into a large glass jar. (Only the teacher may perform this step.)

3. Set the pan of ice on the jar rim and watch what happens.

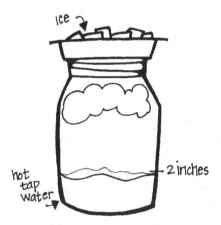

The hot tap water will evaporate, causing water vapor to fill the jar. When the air rises it will run into the cool air at the top of the jar from the metal pan. The cool air will cause the water vapor to condense on the side of the jar and the bottom of the pan.

Activity 23—Rain or Shine

Instructional Materials
♦ *The Cloud Book* by Tomi De Paolo,
♦ *25 Fun Adventure Songs* CD or audiotape,
♦ black construction paper,
♦ tape,
♦ newspaper or gray tissue paper,
♦ stapler,
♦ student journals,

Optional:
♦ *Thunder Cake* book by Patricia Polacco,
♦ gray paint, and
♦ *Thunder Cake* recipe supplies.

Preparation
Set the CD or audiotape to play "I See an Elephant in the Sky." Write the following quote from *The Cloud Book* on the board: "In the morning, mountains, in the evening, fountains."

Background Information
When thunderstorms move in, they typically bring clouds, wind, lightning, and thunder. It can be fun listening to the wind rolling in and the sound of the rain, but it can also be loud and scary.

When cold and warm air meet, the warm air rises and the cold air moves to the bottom. When the warm air moves it takes water vapor with it. The repetition of the movement of the cold and warm air creates a cumulonimbus cloud, or a thunderhead.

Inside this thunderhead is electricity. During storms, clouds become electrically charged, creating the lightning that we see zig-zag down from the clouds. No one really knows why lightning occurs, but it slashes though the air with such a force that it disrupts the air around it. The sound of the air being shoved aside by the lightning is the thunder that follows the flash. It can certainly be loud.

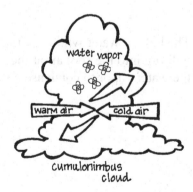

Thunder may be loud, but it can't hurt you. Lightning, on the other hand, is very dangerous. If you get caught in a lightning storm (or electrical storm) seek shelter immediately. If you can't get indoors crouch down, but stay away from the things that lightning is attracted to—like tall trees and poles.

A. Complete the weather chart for the day. Compare the current weather to yesterday's predictions.

B. Read *The Cloud Book* aloud. Ask students to predict what types of clouds are in the pictures before you read each page.

C. Discuss the quote from the book, "In the morning, mountains, in the evening, fountains," using the following questions.
♦ What kind of clouds are like "mountains"? (cumulus)
♦ What kind of weather do "mountains" of clouds bring? (rain)
♦ What do you think the saying means? (If there are fluffy clouds in the morning, by evening it will rain.)
♦ Do you think this saying does a good job forecasting the weather? Why or why not?

D. Ask students to write the rhyming words they found in the book, including hoppin'/droppin,' red/head, tails/sails, gray/way, and mountains/fountains.

E. Ask students to draw in their journals the **cirrus, cumulus, stratus**, and **cumulonimbus** clouds. They should draw the weather they predict next to each cloud.

F. Have students sing "I See an Elephant in the Sky." Then invite them to go outside, lie on their backs, gaze up in the sky, and describe what they see.

G. Share the Background Information about thunderstorms. Show a simple example of thunder in the classroom. Fill a plastic bag with air then stomp on it. Ask students: What happened when the air inside the bag was moved out of the way quickly? You heard a loud pop. When the airwaves are moved by a streak of lightning, you hear a loud clap of thunder.

H. Ask students to write an **onomatopoeia** to describe the sound of thunder in the next blank journal page. Have them write the date at the top, then draw and color a picture of themselves and thunder. Have them answer the following question at the bottom of the page or in the illustration itself: What does the thunder say to you when the lightning crashes down?

I. Ask students to make a thunderhead hat following the instructions on **Thunderhead!**

J. Instruct students to put on their thunderhead hats and divide into lab groups to become a part of a weather "band." Tell students they will work together to identify sounds heard during a rainstorm. Assign each person the task of becoming a sound. Search the classroom for something to symbolize each sound. It can be as simple as tapping on a chair to make the sound of rain. Lab groups work together to create a tune with a combination of their sounds. Students can use their hands, feet, or anything they can find.

Have groups present their music to the class. Band members should identify themselves and the sounds they represent before presenting their tunes. Encourage students to name their bands—like the Fabulous Thunderheads or the Raindrop Rockettes.

K. After everyone has played a tune, list a pattern for the bands to follow and see if they can do it with a little practice. For example:
♦ thunder, thunder, rain, thunder, thunder, wind, thunder, thunder, hail
♦ rain, wind, thunder, rain, wind, thunder, hail, hail, hail
♦ rain, rain, rain, rain, rain, rain, rain, wind, rain, hail, wind (jingle bells)

L. Have students clean up, then allow them to wear their thunderheads home.

M. Ask students to study the weather, predict the next day's weather, and then record the prediction on the weather chart.

Closure
Have students identify what type of clouds they see in the sky today. They should illustrate the types of clouds in their student journals.

Extension
Read aloud *Thunder Cake*. Follow the recipe on the back and share it with the class. Check for any food allergies before serving to students. (If you get lucky and it rains while you are making this recipe, you can pretend to reach outside and catch thunder and pour it into the batter.)

Assessment
Check the Closure activity for accuracy.

Thunderhead!

Instructional Materials
- ◆ black construction paper,
- ◆ stapler,
- ◆ newspaper or gray tissue paper,
- ◆ gray paint,
- ◆ paintbrush, and
- ◆ tape.

Instructions
1. Work with a partner to make a band that fits your head snugly. A sturdy band, double thick folded in half, will work best.

2. Use newspaper to make a large thunderhead cloud. Crunch up papers and connect them with tape. Attach the large cumulonimbus cloud to the headband.

3. Paint the cloud with gray paint and make it look stormy. Add a bolt of lightning with yellow construction paper.

Activity 24—Sun Days

Instructional Materials
- weather chart,
- student journals,
- 1 Meteorology Badges per student,
- crayons or markers,
- scissors, and
- glue.

Preparation
Collect items to demonstrate Earth's orbit around the sun.

Background Information
All weather changes we experience are caused by the sun. Without the sun, Earth would freeze into a ball of ice

The Earth spins on its axis one full circle every 24 hours. This is a full day. We experience day and night in this 24 hours. Obviously, we don't feel like we're spinning around.

While the Earth is spinning on its axis, it is also circling the sun. It takes the Earth a year to complete a circle around the sun. While the Earth is following this circle, known as an orbit, we experience the four seasons—spring, summer, fall, and winter. The tilt of the Earth and its location in orbit cause the sun to heat the atmosphere unevenly around the globe. This causes all the changes in weather we experience. Here's an example: If you stand straight up in front of a campfire, the fire warms you evenly. If you lean toward the campfire, like the Earth on its axis, one part of your body is likely to get warmer than the other. The heat that reaches you body sooner is hotter. The farther it travels, the cooler it gets. These different temperatures around the globe cause a lot of activity in the sky.

A. Complete the weather chart for the day. Compare the current weather to yesterday's predictions.

B. Distribute journals and ask students to divide the next blank page into fourths. Demonstrate how to divide the sheet.

C. Ask students to recall the four seasons, spring, summer, fall, and winter. In square 1, ask students to draw a picture of something that reminds them of spring; in square 2, summer; in square 3, fall; and in square 4, winter. Share pictures and thoughts as a class. Discuss how the weather changes.

D. Have students study the weather outside. Make a final prediction for the next day's weather forecast. Record the prediction on the weather chart. Tell students to check their predictions the next day on TV, in the newspaper, or through another source.

E. Ask students to study the Scientist Skills Cards as a class. Discuss which skills were used to be a meteorologist in the classroom.

Closure

A. Have students draw and label a picture showing the current season. Have them write a complete sentence listing three characteristics that help them determine the season.

B. Have students complete and cut out Meteorology Badges and add them to their Ph.D. diplomas. Congratulate each student.

Extensions

A. Challenge students to create a memory card game with the seasons. Cards could include descriptions of each season, a picture symbolizing each season, the names of each season, etc. Allow time for students to play the memory games after they are created.

B. Help students select a familiar book that is set in one particular season. Challenge students to retell and illustrate the book in the opposite season. Ask them to determine how the story would change if the book were written in a different season.

Assessment

Assess step A of the Closure activity.

Instructional Materials
- ◆ books about the solar system,
- ◆ chalk,
- ◆ 1 Astronomy Badge per student,
- ◆ crayons or markers, and

Optional:
- ◆ a computer with Internet access.

Preparation
Practice singing "9 Little Planets." Make class copies of **Moon Math**.

Background Information
Most people think of the solar system as a huge sun orbited by nine planets. But there's actually much more to it. There are dozens of strange moons, thousands of asteroids, comets, meteorites burning through atmospheres, and even the possibility of other planets beyond Pluto.

There are also black holes, violent asteroid collisions, and storms that measure 40,000 miles across on other planets. Scientists think one of the moons orbiting Jupiter actually rains gasoline.

All this information about the planets is studied and shared with us by scientists called astronomers. Astronomers use physics and mathematics to study the universe—the sun, moon, planets, stars, and galaxies. They study objects millions and even billions of light-years away.

Most astronomers work at universities or colleges, where they often combine teaching and research. About one-third of all astronomers are employed at national observatories or government laboratories such as NASA. Astronomers also work in planetariums, science museums, secondary schools, or in the science journalism field.

A. Ask students if they can think of another science that, like meteorology, requires scientists to look up into the skies. The answer is astronomy. While meteorology is one of the newest of the sciences, astronomy is one of the oldest.

B. Tell students that all **astronomers** have to start with the basics—so this unit begins with our own solar system. Ask students to tell you what they already know about the solar system. Ask if they can name the planets. (Mercury, Venus, Earth, Mars, Jupiter, Saturn, Uranus, Neptune, and Pluto) Ask if they know that the nine planets orbit around the sun.

C. Ask students the following question: Is the sun a star, a planet, an asteroid, or an overgrown orange that fell off a really big tree? (Star) Tell students that the sun is a star at the center of our solar system. Without the sun there would be no planets in orbit. There would be no life.

D. Share the Astronomy Badge and tell students they can begin coloring them in their spare time between projects.

E. Read aloud a book about space to introduce the concept of the solar system.

F. Help students learn the nine planets using **Nine Little Planets.**

G. Teach the order of the planets using a silly sentence. Try this one:

My **V**ery **E**xcited **M**utt **J**umped **S**ixty **U**naware **N**apping **P**oodles

H. Have students use chalk to create a giant map of the solar system on a hard surface outside. Divide students into 10 teams (nine planets and one sun). Have each student draw the sun or one of the planets and share at least two facts about the drawing.

I. Below is the number of moons orbiting each planet. Ask students to order the planets from the least to the most moons.

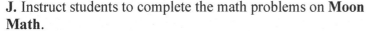

Earth—1 moon	Neptune—8 moons	Saturn—17 moons
Pluto—1 moon	Uranus—15 moons	Venus—no moons
Mars—2 moons	Jupiter—16 moons	Mercury—no moons

J. Instruct students to complete the math problems on **Moon Math**.
Answers:

1. 2
2. 9
3. 13
4. zero
5. zero
6. 1
7. 32
8. 19
9. 16
10. 16

Closure
Ask students to list the order of the planets in their journal. Have each student circle the name of the planet he or she is most interested in.

Extensions

A. Share this Web site with students for current astronomy happenings. As always, please preview any Web site before allowing student access.
http://www.hq.nasa.gov/office/pao/NewsRoom/today.html

B. Divide students into lab groups, then lead them through the instructions below to make a three-dimensional representation of the solar system with papier-mâché. (Butcher paper stuffed with newspaper would also work.)
♦ Rip newspaper into thin strips and dip them in a flour-and-water paste.
♦ Layer paste-covered newspaper strips over wads of newspaper to make planet shapes.
♦ Paint the planets their true colors.
♦ Arrange the sun and planets in order.
♦ Attach a string to each planet.
♦ Hang the planets as a mobile from the ceiling or attach them to a background of black butcher paper along the wall.

Assessment

Assess the Closure activity and check for a basic understanding of the solar system.

Nine Little Planets

Nine little planets circling the sun
Spinning around having so much fun
Mercury said, "I've found my track!"
I'm first in line
You get in   BACK, BACK, BACK
                     BACK, BACK, BACK
                     BACK, BACK, BACK
I'm first in line, you get in back!

Nine little planets circling the sun
Spinning around having so much fun
Venus got in line, "I've found my track!"
I'm second now
You get in   BACK, BACK, BACK
                     BACK, BACK, BACK
                     BACK, BACK, BACK
I'm second now, you get in back!

Nine little planets circling the sun
Spinning around having so much fun
Earth got in place and found its track
I'm third in line
You get in   BACK, BACK, BACK
                     BACK, BACK, BACK
                     BACK, BACK, BACK
I'm third in line, you get in back!

Nine little planets circling the sun
Spinning around having so much fun
Mars got in place and found its track
I'm fourth in line
You get in   BACK, BACK, BACK
                     BACK, BACK, BACK
                     BACK, BACK, BACK
I'm fourth in line, you get in back!

Nine little planets circling the sun
Spinning around having so much fun
Jupiter said, "I've found my track!"

I'm fifth in line
You get in   BACK, BACK, BACK
           BACK, BACK, BACK
           BACK, BACK, BACK
I'm fifth in line, you get in back!

Nine little planets circling the sun
Spinning around having so much fun
Saturn got in line and found its track
I'm sixth in line
You get in   BACK, BACK, BACK
           BACK, BACK, BACK
           BACK, BACK, BACK
I'm sixth in line, you get in back!

Nine little planets circling the sun
Spinning around having so much fun
Uranus got in place and found its track
Seventh is my spot
You get in   BACK, BACK, BACK
           BACK, BACK, BACK
           BACK, BACK, BACK
Seventh is my spot, you get in back!

Nine little planets circling the sun
Spinning around having so much fun
Neptune got in place and found its track
Eighth is my spot
You get in   BACK, BACK, BACK
           BACK, BACK, BACK
           BACK, BACK, BACK
Eighth is my spot, you get in back!

Nine little planets circling the sun
Spinning around having so much fun
Pluto got in line and found its track
I'm ninth in line
HEY, I'm in   BACK, BACK, BACK
           BACK, BACK, BACK
           BACK, BACK, BACK
I'm last in line . . . man, I'm in back!

Moon Math

Instructions

Complete the math problems using the diagram below.

Mercury	0 moons
Venus	0 moons
Earth	1 moon
Mars	2 moons
Jupiter	16 moons
Saturn	17 moons
Uranus	15 moons
Neptune	8 moons
Pluto	1 moon

1. Mercury + Mars = _____

2. Earth + Neptune = _____

3. Uranus – Mars = _____

4. Venus – Mercury = _____

5. Pluto – Earth = _____

6. Jupiter – Uranus = _____

7. Uranus + Saturn = _____

8. Jupiter + Mars + Earth = _____

9. Mercury + Venus + Jupiter = _____

10. Saturn – Jupiter + Uranus = _____

Activity 26—A Star Is Born

Instructional Materials
♦ student journals, and
Optional:
♦ a CD or audiotape of classical music.

Background Information
Stars are balls of burning gases. They form inside clouds of dust and gas called **nebulae**. Small stars are about the size of a large city. Large stars are 100 times bigger than our sun. Stars appear white when we look at them without a telescope, but they are many different colors. The hottest stars are bluish white, the coolest are red, and those between are yellow or orange.

Our star, the sun, is middle-aged at about 4.6 billion years old. It burns yellow-orange and it is estimated that it will live for 5 billion or 6 billion years longer. As it gets older it will expand into space and engulf Mercury and Venus, but it will cool and give off less energy. It will burn a red light. We call stars like these red giants.

From a red giant, a star collapses into a white dwarf and shrinks to the size of one of the smaller plants in our solar system. This star eventually cools and turns into a dark dead star, or a black dwarf. Sometimes larger stars have a more exciting ending. As the cores of larger stars collapse from gravity, they might explode and send their contents flying into space. This is called a supernova. Other large stars may shrink into a black hole where gravity is so strong that not even light can escape.

Astronomers think it takes millions of years for a star to be born. Young stars are big and pale red-orange. As they age, stars get smaller and hotter until they use up the fuel that kept them burning. As stars cool, they swell up. Many scientists think dead stars become **black dwarfs**, with no heat or light, possibly **black holes**, or the largest stars explode in an enormous flash of light called a **supernova**.

A. Ask students to dramatize the life cycle of a star.
♦ Have students spread out in a large area and pull themselves into a ball on the floor waiting to be born.
♦ Read **The Life Cycle of a Star** and have students listen carefully so they can use movement and motions to illustrate the process. Caution students that they will be spinning and turning a lot during this dramatization. If they start getting dizzy, tell them to sit on the floor while moving their upper bodies.

B. Instruct students to draw the life cycle of a star in their journal. Repeat the story as they work.

Closure
Complete the sequencing activity on **Star's Life**.

Extension
Research star patterns called constellations.

Assessment
Assess the Closure activity for accuracy. The correct order is below.

You are dust and gas swirling together.
You start spinning as you grow bigger and redder.
You are blazing hot and can be seen for millions of miles.
You are cooling off.
You explode!

The Life Cycle of a Star

You are a huge cloud of dust and gas, swirling together in a star cloud. You are very active. You feel yourself packing tightly together. Feel the friction! (Rub your hands together.) Feel the heat! You become burning hot. You send out a faint pale-orange glow. You are growing and glowing hotter. Feel the flames lashing out. Feel the energy! (Spin.) You are growing bigger and redder. You are spinning and revolving around other stars, sending your light and energy out through the universe. (Move around the room as you spin.)

You are a blazing hot, blue-white star, full of youthful energy. Spin and orbit in all your glory. Burn, turn! Burn, turn! Burn light! Bright light! Bright light! You are hotter and brighter than anything you can imagine! You are like a young, blue-white hot star. (Turn very fast, with lots of energy.)

You are maturing and mellowing, just a little. (Start to slow down very gradually—little by little.) You still have plenty of energy to give. You are hotter than anything in the solar system. You give forth hot, bright light. Your light can be seen for millions of miles. You shine like a beacon in the sky. You're still a strong, important star.

Spin, turn. Turn, burn! Your color is changing again. Your bright light turns into an electric green-yellow. You are still turning, still orbiting, still heating up the sky. Send out your hot rays. You have energy. Turn, burn.

Spinning, turning. Turning, burning. You have less fuel than when you were young. You are cooling off a bit as you approach old age. Your glow is now a softer, mellow orange. You feel a little bloated. Yes, you are getting fat, like a balloon. Roly-poly, turn, burn. You are a glowing orange ball.

You are cooling as you swell, bigger, bigger! Slower! Slower! You are a red giant. You are inflating as you spin and orbit. (Blow up as you turn and spin.) You are huge. You are important. Look at your giant size now. Who cares if you're no longer heavy and hot and powerful? You're a giant red star. Oh, oh! You look like you'll pop. You feel as if you're going to burst. BOOOOOM! (Collapse on the floor.)

Star's Life

Cut the sentence strips out and arrange them in order.

You are blazing hot and can be seen for millions of miles.

You explode!

You start spinning as you grow bigger and redder.

You are dust and gas swirling together.

You are cooling off.

Activity 27—Solar Power

Instructional Materials
- *25 Fun Adventure Songs* CD or audiotape;
- *student journals;*
- *Why the Sun and the Moon Live in the Sky* book, by Elphinstone Dayrell;
- *Anansi the Spider* book, by Gerald McDermott;

Optional:
- clay;
- straws;
- plastic knife;
- toothpick; and
- manila paper.

Preparation
Set the CD or audiotape to play "The Sun Is So Important." Cut out one sentence strip from **Stars Life** for each student.

Background Information
The sun is the center of the energy that runs the solar system in which we live. **Energy** is made in its center, which is the hottest part. The energy moves out from the center and into the solar system. The sun is so far away that this energy, called solar energy, takes over eight minutes to travel to Earth moving at the speed of light. The energy reaches us as heat and light. Without it, there would be no life on our planet.

A. Ask students to run in place for 30 seconds, then ask the following questions:
- How were you able to run in place? (energy)
- Where did your energy come from? (food)
- Where did the food come from? (store, restaurant, school, or home)
- Where did that come from? (farms or gardens)
- Where do plants get their energy? (the sun)

B. Tell students that the sun is very important to our planet. It provides us with the things we need to survive, such as heat, power, and light.

C. Ask students to fill in the K and W on the K-W-L chart on the sun.

What I Know	What I Think I Know	What I Learned

D. List responses for what students know about the sun under the K column. Include facts (such as the sun is a star), benefits (it makes things grow), and disadvantages (it can cause sunburn). List what students want to learn more about under the W column. Leave the L column blank. Have students fill in this column as they learn new things about the sun. Read aloud **Sun Facts**.

E. Ask students the following questions:
◆ What is the sun? (a star)
◆ What are some things you like to do while out in the sun?
◆ What are some things the sun can do? (Help plants grow, provide power—calculators, cars, heating and electricity systems—give light and heat, illuminate the moon, and so forth.)

F. Teach students the chorus to the song "The Sun Is So Important."

Chorus
The sun is so important.
We could not live without it.
It gives us light.
It helps plants grow.
The sun is so important.

G. Have students listen to the song and sing the chorus.

H. Share the Background Information and read an astronomy book that teaches about the sun.

I. Share some folktales that tell how the Sun got in the sky. Read aloud *Why the Sun and the Moon Live in the Sky* and *Anansi the Spider*.

J. Hand out student journals. Ask students to write or dictate their own folktales about how the sun came to live in the sky. You may choose to create a story as a class.
◆ Sit in a circle.
◆ Display a large piece of chart paper to record the story.
◆ Begin with the first sentence. Moving clockwise around the circle, each student will add another sentence to the story.
◆ Continue until the story is complete. Read the final story aloud. Ask students to illustrate the story in their journals.

K. Complete the K-W-L chart with students.

Closure

A. Ask students to draw a picture in their journals showing why the sun is so important. Have them copy and complete the following sentence in their journals.

The sun is important because ...

B. Ask the following multiple-choice question: What is the sun?
a) a star
b) a planet
c) an asteroid
d) an overgrown orange that fell off a really big tree

Extension

Have students make a sundial and learn how to tell time using the sun. Follow the instructions on **Sundial**.

Assessment

Assess the Closure activity.

Sundial

Instructional Materials
- a straw or a wooden skewer,
- clay,
- a small piece of manila paper,
- a pencil, and
- a toothpick.

Instructions

1. Place the manila paper on the table. Smash the ball of clay onto the middle and stick the straw into the clay so that it is standing straight up.

2. This is your sundial. It is a method created for telling time before clocks were invented. Place your sundial out in the sun. Every hour, go outside and mark the location of the shadow from the straw. Use your toothpick to make a small line in the clay. Mark the time on the paper beside it.

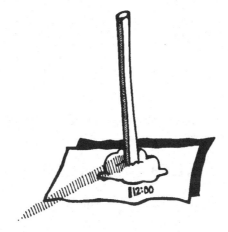

Sun Facts

1. The sun is the center of our solar system.

2. The sun is a middle-aged star that burns bright yellow.

3. The diameter (distance across the sun) is 864,000 miles.

4. The temperature inside the sun is 15 million degrees.

5. Light from the sun takes 8 minutes to get to the Earth traveling at 186,000 miles per second.

6. The sun spins on its axis from left to right.

7. The sun is 4.6 billion years old.

8. The core, the equator of the sun, the top, and the bottom all spin at different speeds.

9. A planet the size of Earth could fit inside the sun more than one million times.

10. The sun's surface, called the photosphere, churns and boils like something in a cooking pot.

11. The sun is not fixed in space. It is constantly moving. It's up to the planets and the moons to keep up as it travels its course.

12. The light that comes from the sun is equal to 4 trillion light bulbs.

13. When the sun was born it was 20 times larger and 100 times brighter than it is today.

14. On Jupiter the sun appears only 1/5 the size of what we see here on Earth.

15. It takes the sun 26 days to spin one time around.

Activity 28—Hold It!

Instructional Materials
♦ bubble liquid and wands;
Optional:
♦ *Astronaut: Living in Space* book, by Kate Hayden; and
♦ student journals.

Preparation
Make or purchase bubbles and bubble wands.

Background Information
Gravity is an invisible force pulling between two objects, and it acts upon all matter throughout the universe. All objects on or near Earth are pulled toward Earth's center until some force or another object intervenes. All objects are affected by gravity. Gravity keeps planets in their orbits and holds people on Earth. It keeps Earth's atmosphere from escaping into space. Gravity is a mystery and one of the least understood concepts in physics.

A. Help students discover gravity by taking turns blowing bubbles and observing what happens. Try to keep the bubbles in the air by blowing on them. Ask students: What continues to pull them down?

B. Ask the following questions:
♦ What did you observe?
♦ What happens to bubbles when you blow on them? Why?
♦ What happens to bubbles when you stop blowing on them?
♦ Why do bubbles fall? (gravity)
♦ What is gravity? (Share the Background Information.)
♦ In what direction does gravity pull on the Earth? (toward the Earth's center)

C. Go outside and let students see how gravity holds the planets in their orbit. Have them follow the steps below.
♦ Choose someone to be the sun.
♦ Everyone else is a planet.
♦ Mark a spot to be the end of the solar system.
♦ Planets form a circle around the sun.
♦ The sun covers his or her eyes and calls "Gravity on!"
♦ All planets circle slowly.
♦ The sun calls "Gravity off!" counts to five, and opens his or her eyes.
♦ The planets walk in a straight line away from the sun before the sun counts to five.
♦ If the sun spots a planet moving, the planet must return to the sun's orbit. The game is over when one planet reaches the end of the solar system.

Optional:
D. Read aloud *Astronaut: Living in Space*.

Closure
Ask students to draw a picture in their journals that shows what life would be like living in a space station without gravity.

Extension
Ask students to locate and read a story about Sir Isaac Newton, one of the first astronomers.

Assessment
Check the Closure activity for accuracy and reasonableness.

Activity 29—New Discoveries

Instructional Materials
- large sheet of butcher paper (preferably white),
- Ph.D. Diploma,
- 1 Astronomy Badge per student, and
- 3 copies of **Building a Solar System.**

Preparation
Collect sheets of butcher paper for each lab group.

Background Information
Astronomy is the study of the planets, stars, solar systems, **galaxies**, and millions of other space bodies that move through the Milky Way and beyond. Astronomers study so many exciting things in space, and there are trillions of things we have yet to discover. Our technology can only take us so far into space. Our telescopes can only see certain distances. Beyond those boundaries it is all up to our imaginations. Beyond our galaxy (the stars we can see) are perhaps billions of other galaxies with other planets orbiting stars.

A. Tell students that even though astronomy is one of the oldest sciences, there is still much more to learn and discover. Share the Background Information.

B. Divide into lab groups and choose Chief Scientists. Give each lab group a large sheet of butcher paper or poster paper. Review **Building a Solar System** with Chief Scientists and the class together. Provide a copy for each group.

C. Have Chief Scientists collect supplies and assign duties for others in their group. Allow groups to work on their project for the remaining class time.

D. Have each group present its new system of planets to the class. The Chief Scientists are in charge of the introduction. Each student must present a planet, two important facts about it, and the calculated distance from the sun.

E. Have students color their Astronomy Badges and add them to their diplomas. Congratulate them on a job well done.

Closure

Review Scientist Skills Cards and discuss how astronomers use each skill as they work.

Extension

Visit a planetarium or invite an astronomer to speak to the class.

Assessment

Assess projects for understanding.

Building a Solar System

Instructional Materials
- butcher paper,
- markers or map pencils,
- crayons,
- a ruler, and
- a pencil.

Instructions

1. Design your own solar system. Create a sun. Determine if your sun is young, middle-aged, or old. This will determine its color. Decide as a lab group which sun you will choose. We call our star the sun. What will you call the star at the center of your solar system? Think of a creative name. Color your star at the center of your piece of paper and write its name out to the side. Remember that the names of things are capitalized.

2. Your solar system should have these components:
- 1 planet per person in your group. The planet should be designed by each individual. It should be colored and named. Write the name to the side of your planet after you draw it on the butcher paper. Decide the location and distance it will be from the sun.
- Calculate a distance from the sun in miles using the scale, 1 inch = 120 million miles.
- On a note card, write two interesting facts about your planet that you will share with the class during the presentation.
- Each planet should have a number of moons per buttons on the outfit you are wearing today. Each moon should have a name and should be smaller than the planet.

3. Work as a group to create a name for the galaxy your solar system is part of. Our solar system is part of the galaxy called the Milky Way. Write the galaxy name at the top of your diagram. This is your title.

4. Present your new system of planets to the classroom. The Chief Scientist is in charge of introducing the diagram. Each student should introduce his or her own planet and read the two interesting facts. All members of the lab group should participate. Don't forget to share the calculated distance from the sun.

Instructional Materials

♦ books about the ocean;
♦ a pair of scissors;
♦ cones, markers, or masking tape for playing area;
♦ 1 wire hanger per student;
♦ yarn (blue or black);
♦ 1 Oceanography Badge per student;

Optional:

♦ *Life in a Tide Pool* book, by Allan Fowler;
♦ an ocean sounds CD or audiotape; and
♦ a seashell collection.

Preparation

Collect wire hangers. Make copies of **Tide 1**, **Tide 2**, and **Tide Patterns** for each student. Make copies of **Tide Treasures**. Make a copy of the Oceanography Badge for each student. Locate a suitable playing area for Treasures in the Tide.

Background Information

Oceanography is the study of the ocean. Scientists who study the ocean are called oceanographers. These scientists spend most of their time on ships learning about the sea. Oceanography focuses on the geological processes taking place under the water, how the ocean and the water react to one another, and how the animals and the sea work together.

The ocean is always moving. Motion is affected by winds, underwater activity such as volcanoes, and currents in the deepest parts of the sea. The motion of the water is also affected by astrological forces, the moon and the sun.

There are two basic kinds of tides. There is **high tide**, also known as flood tide. And there is **low tide**, which is also called ebb tide. High tide and low tide each occur once a day, though they can occur twice in parts of the world. These tides are caused by the gravitational pull of the sun and the moon. Although the sun is bigger, the moon has more effect on the tides because it is closer to Earth.

During low tide, crevices and pools along beaches remain full of water. These are called **tide pools**, and they are home to a variety of ocean life. Some animals are carried in and out with the tides. Creatures living in tide pools include sea anemones, starfish, sand dollars, crabs, and tiny fish.

A. Tell students that their next field of study has a lot to do with astronomy. Explain that oceanographers apply science and technology to the study of the ocean, its contents, and how the ocean is affected by the moon and sun.

B. Share the Oceanography Badge with the class.

C. Ask students to solve the following riddles:

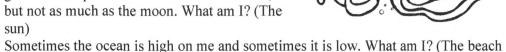

- ◆ I am covered in water and land. Each day and night, the water on me is affected by the sun and moon. What am I? (Earth)
- ◆ I orbit Earth every 24 hours. My gravitational pull causes the oceans to follow me wherever I go. What am I? (The moon)
- ◆ Earth orbits me every 365 days. My gravitational pull has an effect on the oceans, but not as much as the moon. What am I? (The sun)
- ◆ Sometimes the ocean is high on me and sometimes it is low. What am I? (The beach or the shore)
- ◆ When the moon pulls the ocean toward the beach you see me. What am I? (high tide)
- ◆ When the moon is out of sight and the ocean is not pulled toward the beach you see me. What am I? (Low tide)

D. Teach students the following rhyme:

Low tide happens when the moon is out of sight.
High tide happens when the moon is out at night.

E. Read aloud *Life in a Tide Pool* or a book about tides to teach how tides carry life in to the shore and back out to sea.

F. Play a game using **Treasures in the Tide**.

G. Select new Chief Scientists and have lab groups create a tide mobile for their oceanography headquarters. Review the directions on **Tide Mobile** with Chief Scientists while the class is watching. Display completed mobiles in the classroom. Hand out copies of **Tide 1, Tide 2,** and **Tide Patterns** to each student.

Closure
Have students display their mobiles and explain what the symbols represent. Recite the rhyme together as a class. Ask students to share some treasures you might find in a tide pool.

Extensions

A. Ask students to respond to this prompt in their journals: Imagine living months at sea studying the ocean. What might you miss most about being on land?

B. Find a collection of shells, starfish, or sand dollars to share with the class.

C. Discuss how tides affect living creatures on the beach, then ask students to illustrate the effects through writing or drawing. Use the following Web site for further detail. As always, please preview any Web site before allowing student access.
http://www.seaworld.org

Assessment

Assess the Closure activity.

Treasures in the Tide

Instructional Materials
◆ **Tide Patterns** (laminating optional),
◆ scissors,
◆ crayons, and
◆ cones or markers for playing area.

Instructions
1. Use cones, markers, or masking tape to divide an area outside or in a large gym into a large rectangular playing area.

2. One-fourth of the length of the rectangle will represent the beach where the students stroll around. The remaining three-fourths will represent the area where the tides roll in and out.

3. Cut out enough playing pieces from **Tide Treasures**, so every player can collect something that the tide carries in.

4. Ask for two volunteers to play the roles of high tide. These players will stand on the bottom side of the rectangle representing the ocean.

5. Explain the following rules to students. The object is for students on the beach to collect treasures from the tide pools before the high tide comes back in. The students pretending to be high tide will run after the beach strollers standing in the tide area when the teacher yells "high tide." Any strollers caught by the tide have to throw their treasures back into the sea. Students who get back to the beach without getting caught get to keep their treasures. When the teacher yells "low tide" the high tide volunteers have to go back and the beach strollers can begin their search again.

6. Scatter game pieces into the tide area. Begin by calling out "low tide." Call out the tides quickly to keep the game fast-paced. Assign points to tide treasures to make the game a little more interesting.

7. If desired, color game pieces to camouflage them against the background where they will be placed.

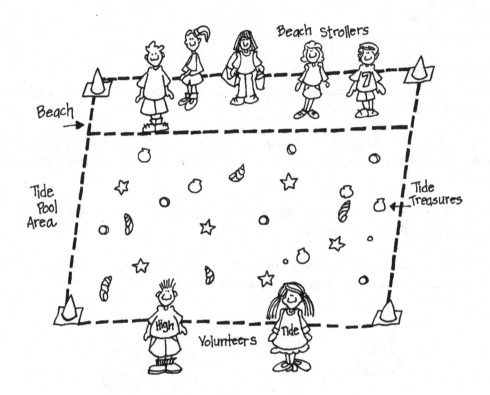

Tide Treasures

Instructions

Make copies of the patterns below. Color, cut, and laminate if desired. Determine the number of copies based on the number of students in the class.

Tide Mobile

Instructional Materials
- 1 wire hanger per student,
- yarn (blue or black),
- crayons or markers,
- tape,
- ruler,
- **Tide Mobile Patterns,**
- scissors, and
- glue.

Instructions

1. Color and cut out **Tide 1** and **Tide 2**. Assemble the two tides by gluing the pieces together. One side represents high tide and the other represents low tide. Color the waves on each side with crayons.

2. Cut out the rhyme on **Tide Mobile Patterns** and glue it to the back of the tide.

3. Attach the tide to the hanger using blue yarn. Follow the illustration below. The high tide should hang 5 inches below the base of the hanger. Make sure the tides hang evenly.

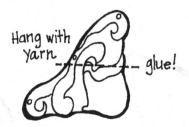

4. Color and cut the other patterns on **Tide Mobile Patterns**. Color the moon and tape it above the high tide on the correct corner of the hanger. Color the sun and clouds and hang them, with yarn, above the low tide. The sun and clouds should balance the mobile. If it is not balanced, create another item to hang with the sun. Maybe a shell or a starfish that you might find at low tide.

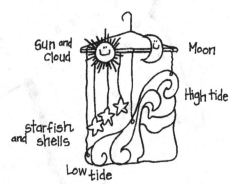

Tide 1

Instructions: Cut out Tide 1 and attach it to Tide 2. Hang the high and low tide from the clothes hanger as instructed.

Glue··· Glue··· Glue··· Glue··· Glue

Tide 2

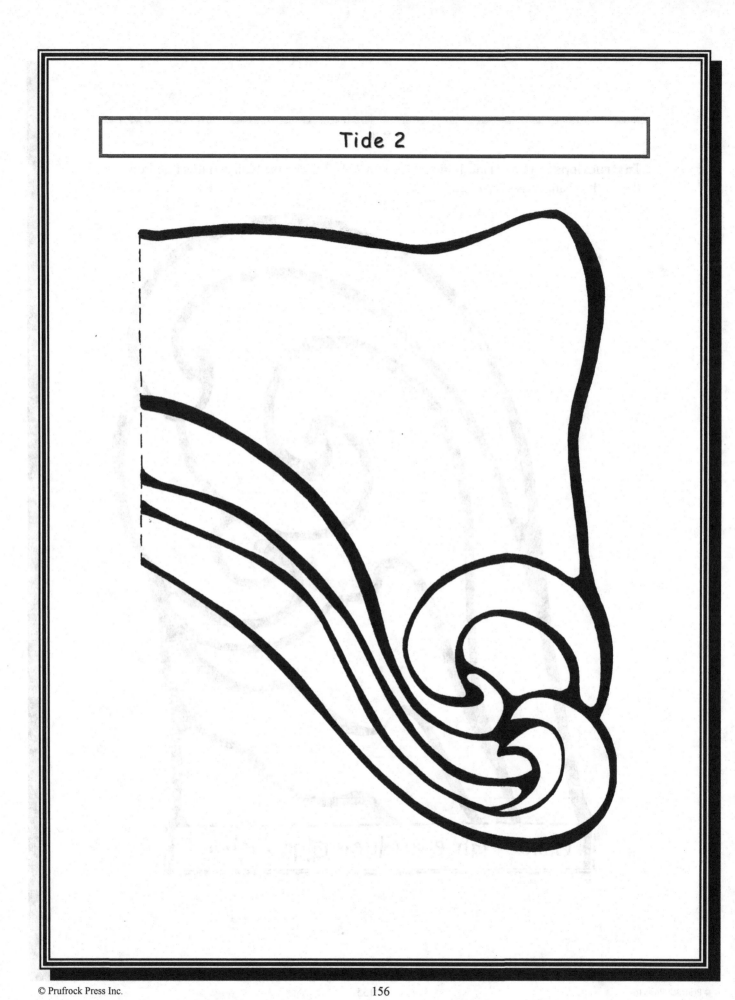

Tide Mobile Patterns

Low tide happens when the moon is out of sight.
High tide happens when the moon is out at night.

Tide Mobile Patterns

Activity 31—Land and Water

Instructional Materials
♦ globe or a large world map;
♦ student journals; and
♦ recycled items, scraps (optional; see the Extension activity).

Preparation
Make 1 copy of **World Map** per student.
Make 1 copy of **Sea Song** per pair of students.
Collect globes or world maps to use for classroom activities

Background Information
The oceans cover about 75 percent of Earth's surface. Studying the ocean is like studying outer space. Both places are mysterious and remote, and scientists need special equipment to survive and perform experiments there. There are four major oceans, the Atlantic, the Pacific, the Arctic, and the Indian. There are many other seas.

A. Distribute copies of the **World Map** to each student. Instruct the class to color all of the land brown and the water blue. Share the Background Information.

B. Hand out journals and have students draw a "T" chart on the next blank page. Instruct them to label the left side of the chart *Ocean* and the right side of the chart *Land*.

C. Ask students to cut the world map into squares following the lines. Explain that if a square has more blue than brown, it should be glued in the *Ocean* column. If the square has more brown than blue, it should go in the *Land* column.

D. Ask students what they can conclude after seeing the results.

E. Teach students the song on **Sea Song**.

F. Ask students to explain the difference between an ocean and a sea. (A sea is a salty body of water that is either part of a larger ocean or landlocked.)

G. Divide students into lab groups. Have Chief Scientists collect a globe or a map of the world and instruct group members to title the next page of their journals "Sea Search." Lab groups will be competing to see how many seas they can locate in 10 minutes. After time has expired, ask groups to name the seas they found. Make a list to see how many the class identified.

Closure
Ask students to locate the nearest ocean or sea.

Extensions
A. Ask students to respond to the following in their journals: If there is so much life on land, imagine how much life must be in the ocean. Make a list of all the sea animals you can think of.

B. Ask students to imagine living in a world with no land. Have them use recycled items and scraps to create a floating house equipped for survival on the ocean.

Assessment
Have students draw a large circle in their journals, then have them create four equal parts by dividing the circle in half twice. Use the following dialogue: You have learned that about 75 percent of the Earth is covered in water. That's about three-fourths of the planet. Color three-fourths of the circle blue to represent the ocean. Color one-fourth of the circle brown to represent land.

World Map

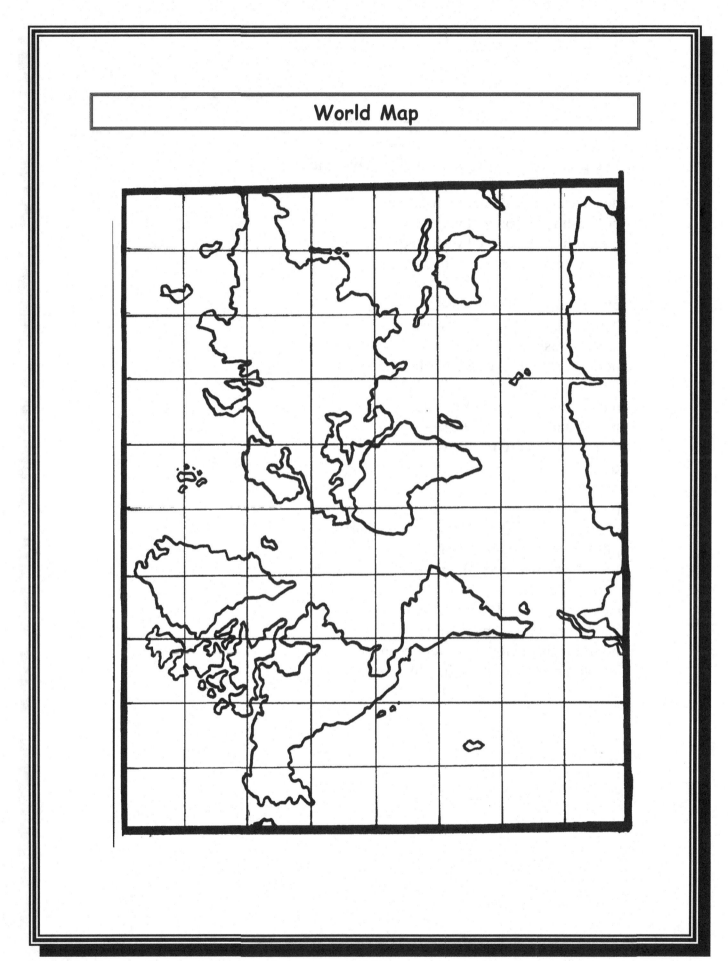

Sea Song

(Sing to the tune of "My Bonnie Lies Over the Ocean.")

The Earth is all covered with water.
The Earth is all covered with sea.
The Earth is all covered with water.
More water on Earth, don't you see?

Splish, splash, splish, splash,
There's water all over the world, the world.
Splish, splash, splish, splash,
There's water all over the world.

So dark and so deep is the water.
So dark and so deep is the sea.
So dark and so deep is the water.
Too dark and too deep, don't you see?

Splish, splash, splish, splash,
There's water all over the world, the world.
Splish, splash, splish, splash,
There's water all over the world.

One ocean is called the Pacific.
Atlantic and Arctic make three.
The Indian is the fourth major ocean.
Now you name them too, just like me!

Activity 32—Wavelengths

Instructional Materials
♦ clear glass baking dish,
♦ plastic test tubes from Test Tube Adventures kits,
♦ blue food coloring,
♦ baby oil,
♦ water,

Optional:
♦ ocean sounds CD or audiotape, and
♦ 1 transparency and 1 copy of **Wave Measurement** per student.

Background Information
Waves have different sizes and strengths. They can be created by wind, earthquakes, volcanoes, and tides. Most waves are caused by wind pulling and pushing the surface of the ocean. The wind's speed, how long it blows, and how far it blows affect the power and size of waves. The top of the wave is called the **crest**. The bottom is called the **trough**. The distance between one crest to the next or from one trough to the next is the **wavelength**.

A **wave** is not like a current. **Currents** move water from one place to another. You can not see currents from the surface of the ocean. Oceanographers measure the motion of the water underneath the sea to find currents. A wave is visible from the surface, but a wave is not moving water. A wave is a rise and fall of ocean water as energy is transferred from one place to another. As the wave gets closer to shore, the bottom starts to drag along the ocean floor. As this happens the bottom of the wave starts to slow down, but the top of the wave keeps moving forward. It gets so far ahead that it falls over and breaks onto the beach.

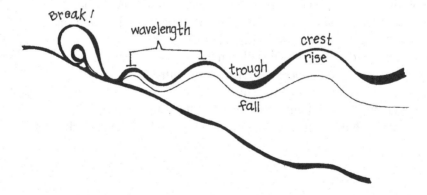

A. Review how tides are created. Tell students that the tide comes in waves. Ask students what they know about waves. Share the Background Information.

B. Students observe waves using an overhead projector and a glass baking dish containing water.

♦ Place the baking dish on the overhead projector and turn the projector on.
♦ Allow the water to settle, and then touch the center of the water with your finger. Have students describe to a neighbor what happens.
♦ Allow the water to settle again, and then drop a small object into the center of the water. Have students describe to a neighbor what happens.
♦ Ask what caused the wave. (Touching the surface of the water.) This is how waves are formed at the surface. The wind touches the water and causes it to move in a circular motion.
♦ Allow the water to settle. Delicately drop one drop of blue food coloring into the center of the water.
♦ Drop a small object into the center of the water and watch the wave action move the blue food coloring.

C. Have students work in three lab groups to re-create a wave, using instructions below.
♦ Fill a tube half full of water. (Get help from the teacher if needed.)
♦ Add several drops of blue food coloring and mix well by screwing on the cap and gently shaking.
♦ Fill the rest of the tube with baby oil. Try not to let any air remain inside the bottle.
♦ Screw on the cap tightly, and take turns tilting the bottle gently to the right and left. If the mixture becomes foamy, let it sit for a few minutes so the alcohol and oil can separate.

D. Complete **Wave Measurements** together as a class. Make a transparency to use on the overhead.

E. Instruct students to make a human wave to learn the parts of a wave.
♦ Ask students to join hands in a circle, then show them how to raise and lower one arm to simulate a wave.
♦ Have students pass the wave to one another by raising and lowering arms.
♦ Discuss how the wave goes up and down and around the circle.
♦ Remind students that the top of the wave is called the crest and the bottom part is called the trough. The distance between two consecutive crests or troughs is called the wavelength. When waves are way out in the ocean, their wavelengths are usually longer than when a wave nears a shoreline.
♦ Have students create a human wave again, this time shouting "Crest!" when their hands are up and "Trough!" when their hands are down.

Closure

Ask students to draw a wave in their journals. They should label the crest with an X and the trough with an O. Have students draw a dotted line from crest to crest and trough to trough to identify the wavelength.

Extensions

A. Encourage teams of students to write a song that teaches about crests, troughs, and wavelengths. Have them choose a familiar tune to which to write, such as "Twinkle, Twinkle, Little Star."

B. Have teams present their songs to the class.

Assessment

Assess the Closure activity.

Wave Measurement

1. What is the wavelength? Use your ruler to measure the distance between the two crests.

2. What is the wavelength? Use your ruler to measure the distance between the two troughs.

3. Which of the above waves would most likely be closer to shore? Why?

4. Which of the above waves would most likely be farther from shore? Why?

Activity 33—Jacques Cousteau

Instructional Materials
- books or references about Jacques Cousteau,
- scissors,
- crayons or markers,
- stapler, and

Optional:
- a computer with Internet access.

Preparation
Make 1 copy of **The Story of Jacques Cousteau** book per student.

Background Information
Jacques Cousteau was the world's most famous oceanographer. He was born in 1910 and became a French naval officer, marine explorer, author, and documentary filmmaker. Cousteau was serving in the French navy when he began his underwater explorations. In 1943, he and French engineer Emile Gagnan perfected the aqualung, a cylinder of compressed air connected through a pressure-regulating valve to a facemask. (The aqualung is also called scuba gear.) The aqualung enabled divers to stay underwater for several hours. Cousteau died in 1997.

A. Ask students if they have ever heard of Jacques Cousteau. Tell them that he was the most famous oceanographer, then share the Background Information.

B. Give each student a copy of **The Story of Jacques Cousteau**. Read the story together. Ask students to reread the story aloud to a partner.

C. Instruct students to color the illustrations, then put the book together in correct order.

D. Ask students to read the book aloud in unison.

Closure
Ask the following comprehension questions:
- Why did Cousteau begin swimming? (to build up his strength)
- What did he join when he grew up? (the French navy)
- What did he help invent? (the aqualung)

- Why was this important? (It helped people stay under water longer so they could discover more about the sea.)
- What do people call the aqualung today? (scuba gear)
- What did Cousteau help people around the world do? (see under the sea)

Assessment
Assess the Closure activity.

Extensions
A. Rent one of Jacques Cousteau's videos and show a few clips to the class. Or check out the Cousteau Web site below. As always, please preview any Web site before allowing student access.
www.cousteau.org

B. Ask for a volunteer who has scuba equipment to demonstrate how the gear works.

The Story of Jacques Cousteau

Jacques Cousteau was often sick as a child.

He learned to swim so he could get strong.

He loved the water. He loved the sea.

He wanted to know all about it.

He joined the French navy as soon as he could.

He helped make a machine that allows people to stay under the water longer. This machine was called an aqualung.

Today people call it scuba gear.

Jacques figured out how to make movies underwater.

He helped people around the world learn about the world under the sea.

Activity 34—Sea Creatures

Instructional Materials

- ocean reference books;
- butcher paper (3 rectangular pieces of equal size: 1 light blue, 1 dark blue, 1 black);
- paint;
- markers;
- crayons;
- scissors;
- glue;
- construction paper (other recycled items for crafts); and

Optional:

- a computer with Internet access.

Background Information

The ocean is divided into three layers: the sunlight zone, the twilight zone, and the midnight zone. The **sunlight zone** is home to 90 percent of marine life in the ocean. It extends from the surface to between 300 and 600 feet below the surface. The **twilight zone** begins around 600 feet below the surface and ends about 3,000 feet below the surface. Below this is the midnight zone, also called the **abyssal zone**. It makes up approximately three-fourths of the ocean. It begins where the twilight zone ends and continues to the ocean floor. The depth of the majority of the ocean is still unknown. Oceanographers use a system of echolocation to measure the distance to the bottom of the sea. Echolocation is the process of sending out sound waves to see what something looks like. Some ocean animals use echolocation to find food. It will take another 100 years to map the entire ocean. An ichthyologist is a scientist who studies fish.

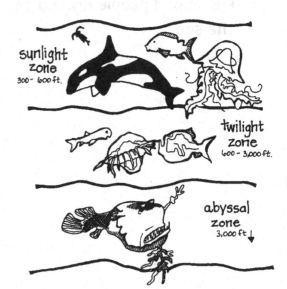

A. Select new Chief Scientists and place a different color of butcher paper in front of each lab group. Ask the following question: As you can see, I have selected a different color of butcher paper for each lab group. How do these colors relate to the ocean?

B. Discuss answers then share the Background Information on the layers of the ocean. Have students help you brainstorm what they would find at the three layers of the ocean. Ask which layer their colors represent.

C. Discuss why certain sea creatures are better suited to one of the three layers or can only live in one of the layers. For example, whales must come up to the surface for air in order to stay alive, and sponges cannot move so they must stay fixed to the bottom, where they can collect food, etc.

D. Assign each lab group to one layer of the ocean. Have them research creatures, plants, or other inhabitants in their layer. Have students create the environment using paint, construction paper, glue, markers, and crayons.

E. Tape the layers to the wall, in order, to create a mural of the ocean. Label each layer.

Closure
Ask students to draw in their journals three layers of the ocean, then label each layer, then place one sea creature in each layer.

Extensions
A. Instruct students to research the cookie cutter shark and learn about bioluminescence. Have students paint a picture of a bioluminescent fish using glow-in-the-dark paint.

B. To learn more about creatures in the sea, visit the Web site. As always, please preview any site before allowing student access.
http://www.sciencenews.org/sn_arc98/8_1_98/fo

Assessment
Assess the Closure activity. Ask students to explain why each sea creature drawn in the journal belongs in that particular ocean layer.

Activity 35—Thar She Blows!

Instructional Materials
- reference books about whales;
- tape measures or yardsticks;
- *25 Fun Adventure Songs* CD or audiotape;
- 1 Oceanography Badge per student;
- large, clear measuring cup;
- oatmeal, small pasta, granola (or other small material to pass through a strainer);
- water; and
- a strainer.

Preparation
Set the CD or audiotape to play "Blue Whale, Blue Whale."

Background
Whales live in the sunlight zone of the ocean because they require air to survive. Whales usually come to the surface to breathe every 10 minutes. Whales breathe through a blowhole on the top of their heads or on their backs. They can't breathe through their mouths, because they don't have a hole going to their lungs. This makes it easier for them to eat. There are two types of whales: toothed and baleen.

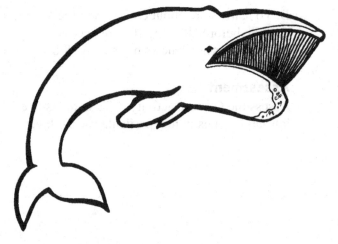

Even though they live in the ocean, whales are mammals, not fish. Many whales live near the polar regions where the water is extremely cold. Because they are warm-blooded animals, they have a thick coat of blubber that keeps them warm in these extreme temperatures. In warm-blooded animals, body temperatures stay about the same regardless of outside temperatures. The blubber on these whales is usually 12 inches thick.

Dolphins are closely related to toothed whales. They are also warm-blooded mammals. A relative of the dolphin is the porpoise. The porpoise has a nose that is more blunt and is smaller than a dolphin's.

Fish are cold-blooded animals so their body temperatures change or adapt to the temperature of the water they live in.

A. Ask students what the largest animals on Earth are (Blue whales). Ask which layer of the ocean these animals live in (Sunlight).

B. Ask students how whales are different from other sea creatures in their mural. (Whales are mammals, just like humans.) Ask students what whales, humans, and other mammals have in common. (They have live babies instead of eggs, feed their babies milk, are warm-blooded, and have hair. Whales have whiskers that are considered hair.)

C. Have the three lab groups each walk off what they estimate to be the length of a blue whale. See which group comes the closest to 100 feet, the approximate length of a blue whale. Ask students to determine how many of their body lengths would equal the length of a blue whale. Then have them write their estimations in their journals. Ask students to figure out how many of their teachers would fit into the length of a blue whale.

D. Instruct students to estimate how long the following lengths are then measure to see how close they came. Using trial and error, each attempt should be better than the last.

fin whale	80 feet
humpback whale	60 feet
gray whale	50 feet
orca (killer whale)	30 feet
pilot whale	26 feet
narwhal	15 feet
dolphin	7 feet

E. Tell students that the blue, fin, humpback, and gray whales don't have teeth. They have baleen instead. Baleen whales gulp great mouthfuls of water and krill (tiny, shrimp-like animals). They use their tongues and cheeks to push the water through the long plates of **baleen**, trapping the krill inside. (It's like a strainer for pasta.) The whale then licks up the krill, swallows, and gulps again. A blue whale eats 8,000 pounds of krill in a day.

F. Demonstrate how baleens work. Fill a large measuring cup with water. Add oatmeal, granola, and other small items that will catch in a strainer. Tell students as you pour the contents through the strainer that the whale pushes the water out, leaving the food behind.

G. Have students listen to "Blue Whale, Blue Whale" and learn the chorus:

Blue whale, blue whale,
swimming in the sea,
catching all the little krill,
with your special baleen,

Blue whale, blue whale,
you eat tons each day—
for you need to feed your little calf
before you two can play.

H. Have students write and complete the following sentence in their journals:

The biggest animal in the world is the _____.

I. Ask students to draw the whale in their journals.

Closure
Give each student an Oceanography Badge. Congratulate students on completing this unit of study. Have students complete their badges and glue them to their diplomas.

Extensions
A. Ask students to create a bar graph comparing the lengths of different whales. Have them color the baleen whales one color and toothed whales another color. Ask them: What can you conclude by looking at these comparisons?

B. Have students finish these generalizations:

The bigger the whale, the less likely it is to have _____ (teeth).
The smaller the whale, the more likely it is to have _____ (teeth).
Bigger whales eat smaller _____ (prey, or food).

Assessment
Assess the journal entry asking which animal is the world's largest.

Activity 36—Classification

Instructional Materials
♦ reference books about animals;
♦ *25 Fun Adventure Songs* CD or audiotape;
♦ *Baby Whales Drink Milk* book, by Barbara Juster Esbensen;
♦ student journals;
♦ 1 Zoology Badge per student; and
Optional:
♦ *Tuesday* book, by David Wiesner.

Preparation
Make a transparency of **Classification Chart** or re-create the chart on the board.

Background
Zoology is the study of the animal kingdom. Zoology encompasses many fields of study because there are thousands of animal species. Entomologists are zoologists who specialize in studying insects. Ornithologists specialize in studying birds, ichthyologists specialize in fish, etc.

All animals have three things in common: They move or have some way to travel, they have to find food, and they are made of living cells that keep them alive. Animals are divided into two categories: vertebrates (animals with a backbone) and invertebrates (animals with no backbone).

Mammals are a class in the animal kingdom. Mammals give birth to live babies, feed their young with milk from their bodies, and have hair. Mammals are warm-blooded vertebrates.

Reptiles and amphibians are part of the animal kingdom also. A zoologist who studies them is called a herpetologist. **Reptiles** are animals with dry, scaly skin that breathe by means of lungs. There are about 6,000 kinds of reptiles, and they make up one of the classes of vertebrates. Reptiles include alligators, crocodiles, lizards, snakes, and turtles. Characteristics of reptiles include thick, scaly skin, and three-chambered heart.

About 4,200 species of frogs, toads, salamanders, and caecilians make up the **amphibian** group of animals. Almost all amphibians have legs, all breathe with lungs as well as through their skin, and they all have a heart that is divided into three chambers. The major difference between reptiles and amphibians is that an amphibian must return to water to lay its soft, jelly-like eggs. Reptiles lay their hard-shelled eggs on land.

A. Tell students that at some point a zoologist determined that a whale was a mammal and not a fish. It is part of a zoologist's job is to classify animals. Ask the following question: How did a zoologist come to the conclusion that a whale is not a fish?

B. Share the Zoology Badge with the class. Allow students to work on the badge during their free time.

C. Read aloud *Baby Whales Drink Milk*.

D. Ask students if they are vertebrates or invertebrates. Have everyone reach behind and feel their backbones running down their necks past their hips. Ask students: What other animals have backbones? (Dogs, cats, birds, fish, snakes.) What animals have no backbones? (Starfish, sponges, mollusks, squid, clams, octopus, sand dollars, etc.)

E. Review with students that an entomologist is a zoologist who specializes in insects. Ask students to recall what classifies an animal as an arthropod and fill in the first column of **Classification Chart**. (Exoskeleton, invertebrate, three body parts, two compound eyes, two antennae or feelers, and six jointed legs.)

F. Ask students to recall what classifies an animal as a mammal and fill in the second column on the chart. (They have live babies instead of eggs, feed their babies milk, have hair, and are warm-blooded.) Have students recall information from *Baby Whales Drink Milk*.

G. Ask students to use deductive reasoning and prior knowledge to figure out what characteristics are common for amphibians and reptiles. Share the Background Information.

H. Sing "What Are Amphibians?" from *25 Fun Adventure Songs*.

I. Go outside and play a game of leapfrog.

Optional:

J. Share the book *Tuesday*. Make careful note of the times given randomly through the story. Ask students to estimate what time it might have been when the frogs were watching TV with Grandma. Ask students how they got their answers.

Closure

Ask students to create a T-chart in their journals dividing animals into vertebrate and invertebrate groups. Provide magazines with pictures of animals for students to cut out.

Extensions

A. Have students make up riddles to ask their lab groups. For example: I am a vertebrate, I have legs, and I lay my eggs in the water. What am I? (Amphibian or frog.)

B. Sing "If Only I Could Leave My Shell" from *25 Fun Adventure Songs*.

C. Go on a tadpole hunt or purchase some from a pet store and watch their life cycle.

Assessment

Assess the Closure activity for accuracy.

Classification Chart

	Arthropods	Mammals	Reptiles	Amphibians
Backbone				
Live young/eggs				
Hair				
Exoskeleton				
Number of legs				
Eyes				
Other				

Activity 37—Observations

Instructional Materials
♦ student journals, and

Optional:
♦ a CD or audiotape of animal sounds.

Preparation
Arrange for students to observe an animal or group of animals. This could be anything from a hamster in a cage, fish in a bowl, ants, birds or squirrels on the playground, or a group of children at recess. It would be great if you could arrange three observation areas and divide students into three lab groups so they can rotate and make three observations. Make a transparency of Animal Observations. Make classroom copies of Animal Analogies, Fact and Opinion, and Animal Body Language.

Background Information
Zoologists specialize in learning all they can about particular animals. They study the animal habitats, life cycles, language, physical traits, and environmental effects. They do this so they can share their knowledge to protect people and animals.

Zoologists like to make observations in the wild. This can be exciting and dangerous. They make special trips to study animals for months at a time. They may go on safaris or deep-sea expeditions, or they may just walk into the woods behind their homes. Some observe animal behavior at zoos. Here, animals in captivity are studied and taken care of in their home away from home. New babies are born to species that are on the brink of extinction and cared for.

A. Tell students that one important part of being a zoologist is learning to make careful observations. This is how they understand the ways animals communicate, what they eat, how they move, where they live, how certain things affect them like noise, weather, and temperature. This not only helps zoologists know how to best care for animals, but it also helps them protect themselves.

B. Hand out student journals. Ask students to copy the following question in their journals:

What animal sounds would you recognize without seeing what made the noise?

C. Have students bring their lists to the large group. Ask for volunteers to share some of the animals they listed in their journal. Make the animal sounds together.

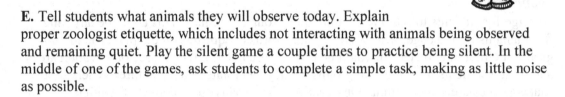

D. Share **Animal Body Language Chart** with the class. Explain that body language is a way most animals communicate when not using their voices. Read the chart together, and then ask students how knowing this information might help a zoologist protect him- or herself. Ask if they can add to the chart.

E. Tell students what animals they will observe today. Explain proper zoologist etiquette, which includes not interacting with animals being observed and remaining quiet. Play the silent game a couple times to practice being silent. In the middle of one of the games, ask students to complete a simple task, making as little noise as possible.

F. Distribute one copy of **Animal Observations** to each student. Make sure everyone has a pencil and a hard surface on which to write. A clipboard would work well.

G. Begin the observation. This can last as long as you think there is good learning going on. This can be an ongoing observation or just one time.

H. Share the following with students: Observations are sometimes part fact and part opinion. A **fact** is something known to be true. An **opinion** is an idea or belief that a person thinks is true. For example, a scientist observing a grizzly bear might note the fact that the bear is brown. But a scientist might also form opinions based on observations or body language. For example, the bear looked like he might be agitated and hungry.

I. Instruct students to complete **Fact and Opinion**.

J. Ask students to check their animal observation charts and try to distinguish between facts and opinions.

Closure

Discuss observations. Make sure students don't overgeneralize. One hamster might like a paper towel roll to sleep in while another may not. Emphasize that before zoologists or any scientists can announce a discovery or form a conclusion (like writing the animal body language chart) they have to observe many animals, many times, in many circumstances.

Extension

Practice the analogies using **Animal Analogies**.
Answers:

1. oink
2. egg
3. foal or colt
4. school
5. walk or run
6. hop or leap
7. small
8. water
9. bird
10. sing or chirp
11. jungle

Assessment

Check the observation chart for accuracy and notes.

Animal Body Language

Animal	Body Language
dog	- Its tail straight up in the air means back off. - Lying on its back with ears flat to its head and its tail tucked shows it thinks you're the boss. - Tucking the tail under the body shows fear.
cat	- An arched back and puffed-up fur to appear larger means the cat is frightened. - Purring means the cat is happy. - Meowing loudly means it wants to be put down.
peacock	- Spreading its tail feathers means it's trying to attract a mate and show off to other peacocks.
chimpanzee	- A chimp opens its mouth and bares its teeth to show anger.
rabbit	- A rabbit thumps its foot on the ground when frightened.

Animal Observations

Date:

Time: (when you start the observation and when you finish)

Animal: (what is being observed)

Environment: (natural environment like an anthill or **artificial** environment like a bowl or cage)

Experiment or condition: (are you going to feed the animal, alter its environment, or make other changes?)

Notes: (words or pictures)

ANIMAL	FACT	OPINION
Fact and Opinion		
FROG		
BEAR		
DOG		
CAT		
BIRD		
SNAKE		
FISH		
WHALE		
SHARK		

Animal Analogies

Instructions
Fill in the blank with the correct analogy.

1. Duck is to quack as pig is to _____.

2. Cow is to milk as hen is to _____.

3. Bear is to cub as horse is to _____.

4. Wolf is to pack as fish is to _____.

5. Fish is to swim as human is to _____

6. Snake is to slither as frog is to _____.

7. Elephant is to big as mouse it to _____.

8. Monkey is to tree as hippo is to _____.

9. Poodle is to dog as blue jay is to _____.

10. Wolf is to howl as bird is to _____.

11. Bear is to forest as monkey is to _____.

Activity 38—Poetic Zoologists

Instructional Materials
♦ student journals; and
Optional:
♦ *Animal Tracks* book, by Arthur Durros.

Preparation
Make a transparency of Animal Songs or make one copy for each pair of students.

A. Sing the animal songs as a class.

B. Ask students to identify the pattern in the song. Write the pattern on the board.

I'm a _____. I'm a _____.

See my _____. See my _____.

_____ through the tall _____.

_____ through the tall _____.

Looking for _____. Looking for _____.

C. Distribute journals and divide students into lab groups. Ask students to work together to write two more verses using the pattern.

D. Write the following words on the board: *finch, mockingbird, eagle, ostrich.*

E. Ask students if they can figure out the pattern. (Smallest to largest.) Try another pattern, such as alphabetical order.

F. Challenge students to come up with their own patterns and share them with the class.

Closure
Ask students what the patterns are called that animals leave when they travel. (Tracks.) Instruct students to design a pattern of animal tracks in their journals. Tell students to write a sentence at the bottom that tells what your animal was doing while making the tracks. Remind students that patterns repeat themselves.

Extensions

A. Read aloud *Animal Tracks*.

B. Have students complete The Missing Story.

Assessment

Check the Closure activity for a pattern.

Animal Songs

(Sing to the tune of "Frere Jacques.")

I'm an eagle. I'm an eagle.
See my wings. See my beak.
Flying through the tall trees.
Soaring through the tall trees.
Looking for a mate. Looking for a mate.

I'm a snake. I'm a snake.
See my tongue. See my scales.
Sliding through the tall grass.
Gliding through the tall grass.
Looking for lunch. Looking for lunch.

I'm a cheetah. I'm a cheetah.
See my teeth, See my claws.
Creeping through the tall grass.
Slipping through the tall grass.
I am fast. I am fast.

I'm a zebra. I'm a zebra.
See my stripes. See my mane.
Galloping through the tall grass.
Jumping through the tall grass.
Running from lions. Running from lions.

I'm a bullfrog. I'm a bullfrog.
See my tongue. See my eyes.
Hopping through the tall grass.
Jumping through the tall grass.
Looking for bugs. Looking for bugs.

The Missing Story

Instructions

Study each equation below. Write a word problem in the space provided to tell an animal story about each subtraction and addition problem.

Animal Word Problem 1

$5 + 4 = 9$

Animal Word Problem 2

$7 - 2 = 5$

Animal Word Problem 3

$8 + 8 = 16$

Animal Word Problem 4

$10 - 5 = 5$

Animal Word Problem 5

$5 + 9 = 14$

Activity 39—Research Fun

Instructional Materials
- library books and assorted references on animals,
- old socks,
- paper bags,
- double-sided mounting tape,
- scrap felt or art foam,
- construction paper (assorted colors),
- yarn (assorted colors),
- miscellaneous recycled items or craft supplies (for puppet making),
- glue,
- scissors, and
- crayons, markers, or colored pencils.

Preparation
Divide supplies evenly among lab groups. Locate the zoo nearest you. Provide the address and phone number, and a map if available, for students to share with their families.

A. Tell students that today they will research the animal of their choice, then have them make a puppet of the animal.

B. Ask students to write five facts about their animals in their journals.

C. At the end of the day, have students share their puppets and research.

Closure
Have students share information about the nearest zoo and plan a trip with their families.

Extension

Discuss the intended and the literal meanings of the below idioms with students, then have them illustrate their favorites.

- ◆ Don't be such an animal!
- ◆ It's raining cats and dogs!
- ◆ I've got butterflies in my stomach.
- ◆ His bark is worse than his bite.
- ◆ She's gone batty!
- ◆ The cat's got his tongue.
- ◆ Birds of a feather flock together.
- ◆ Don't be such a scaredy cat.

Assessment

Assess understanding of facts and opinions by reviewing research in student journals.

Activity 40—Animal Games

Instructional Materials
- ♦ manila paper (small size—per student),
- ♦ pencil,
- ♦ scissors,
- ♦ stapler,
- ♦ bathroom scale, and
- ♦ a calculator.

Preparation
Make 1 copy of **Rounding up the Herd** per two students.
Make an elephant ear pattern for each lab group.

Background
Elephants are enormous animals of extreme intelligence. Elephants live (in the wild) in Africa and Asia, and travel in herds of up to 25. Elephants are nomads, which means they will travel hundreds of miles to find food. They eat grasses, leaves, fruits, and nuts. There are two kinds of elephants. The African elephant has large ears and very wrinkled skin. Its ears are actually shaped like the continent of Africa, and each one can weigh up to 110 pounds. The Asian elephant, also known as the Indian elephant, has smaller ears and much smoother skin.

A. Share the Background Information with students. Weigh or estimate each student's weight and record the information on the board. Find out how many students it would take to equal the weight of an elephant ear. What about two ears?

B. Tell students the following: An elephant can weigh up to 15,400 pounds. What's the total weight of everyone in our classroom? Do we weigh as much as an elephant put together? (Use a calculator.)

C. Teach a lesson on rounding numbers to the nearest 10 or 100. Have students complete **Rounding up the Herd** in a group or partners.
Answers:

1. 60	6. 200	11. 600
2. 1,000	7. 900	12. 70
3. 120	8. 80	13. 20
4. 200	9. 30	
5. 10	10. 40	

D. Have lab groups make elephant ears using **Elephant Ears**.

E. Congratulate students on becoming amateur zoologists. Allow students to complete their Zoology Badges and add them to their diplomas.

F. Review Scientist Skills Cards, and ask students to determine how a zoologist uses each of the skills.

Closure

Ask students to list what they have learned about zoology.

Extensions

A. Ask students to review the Scientist Skills Cards and order them from most used skill to least used skill by zoologists.

B. Ask students to be prepared to explain their answers.

Assessment

Assess the Closure activity.

Rounding up the Herd

Instructions

Read each sentence. Round the number to the nearest 10 or 100. Record your answer in the blanks provided.

1. There were 57 wolves in the pack. Round to the nearest 10. _____

2. There were 1,001 bees in the hive. Round to the nearest 100. _____

3. There were 122 fish in the school. Round to the nearest 10. _____

4. There were 176 geese in the flock. Round to the nearest 100. _____

5. There were 5 members in the family. Round to the nearest 10. _____

6. There were 247 wildebeest in the herd. Round to the nearest 100. _____

7. There was a stream of 894 minnows. Round to the nearest 100. _____

8. There was a swarm of 82 grasshoppers. Round to the nearest 10. _____

9. There were 28 hammerheads. Round to the nearest 10. _____

10. There was a party of 42 for dinner. Round to the nearest 10. _____

11. There were 611 swordfish in the company. Round to the nearest 100.

    ____

12. There were 71 monkeys. Round to the nearest 10. _____

13. There were 18 cave bears in the clan. Round to the nearest 10.

    _____

Elephant Ears

Instructional Materials
- gray construction paper
- scissors,
- stapler or glue,
- **Africa Pattern,** and
- a pencil.

Instructions

1. Trace 2 patterns of Africa on gray construction paper. These will be the elephant ears. Remember one will flip over to make the other ear.

2. Cut a band to fit around your head. Have a partner help you make the correct size so it fits well.

3. Attach an elephant ear from **Africa Pattern** to each side using a stapler.

4. Wear your African elephant ears around the classroom.

Africa Pattern

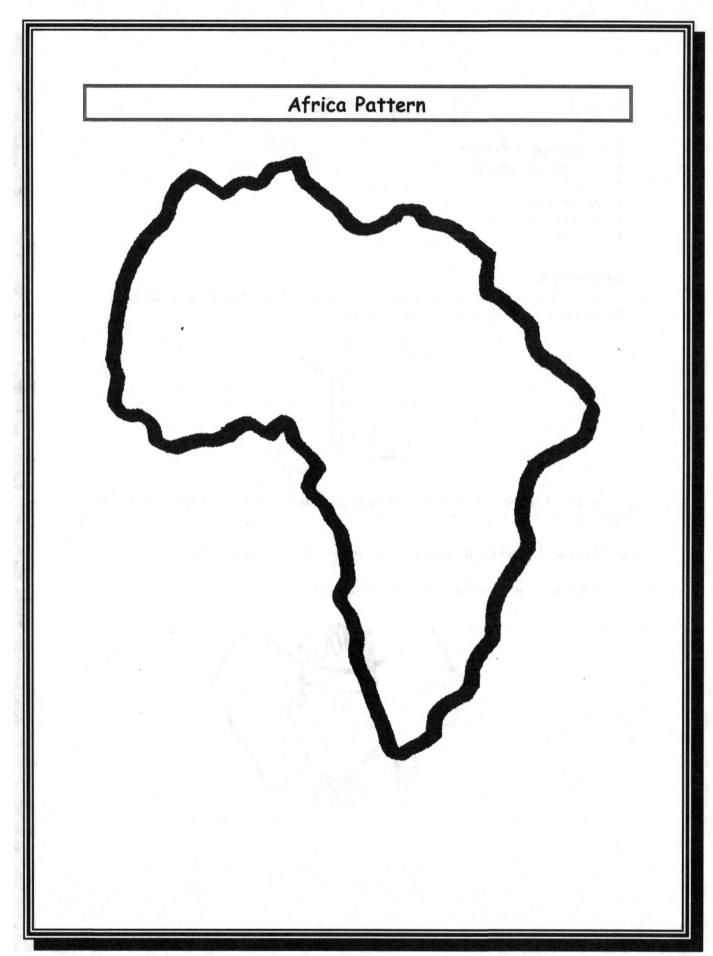

Activity 41—Paleontology

Instructional Materials
- *25 Fun Adventure Songs* CD or audiotape;
- paint (shades of brown);
- paintbrushes;
- 1 copy of Paleontologist Tools per student;

Optional:
- aluminum foil (small square per student);
- (1) 5-inch piece of rope per student; and
- *Digging up Dinosaurs* book, by Aliki; *Dinosaur's Day* book, by Ruth Thomson; *Dinosaur World* book, by Christopher Santoro; *Dinosaurs Are Different* book, by Aliki.

Preparation
Send a note home asking parents to send an old shoe box or a box of similar size (but no larger) for a paleontology activity. Save the shoe box lid for Activity 46.

Background Information
Paleontology is the study of fossils and other ancient life forms. A scientist who studies paleontology is called a paleontologist. To become a paleontologist you have to study science, especially biology and geology. Biology is the study of living things. **Geology** is the study of the Earth's layers of soil and rock. Paleontologists search for **fossils** and study rock layers as they dig, providing other scientists with valuable information and land maps. Using fossils and dating methods, they are able to determine the ages of certain layers of the Earth. These maps help in the search for oil, water, and minerals.

Dinosaurs are thought to be descendents of the reptile family. From fossil remains, paleontologists have determined that dinosaurs first began roaming the Earth about 230 million years ago. Reptiles are cold-blooded animals whose body temperatures adjust to the surrounding air. Some dinosaurs may have also been warm-blooded, so their body temperature stayed the same year round, like ours. Dinosaurs varied greatly in size. Some were as small as a house cat. Some were as large as a jet. Remains found at dig sites could include bones, egg shells, bone fragments, teeth, fossilized plants, imprints, and dung.

A. Explain that paleontologists are zoologists who study the remains of prehistoric life and fossils that no longer exist. Ask students to brainstorm animals that no longer exist. Remind students this is called being **extinct**.

B. Ask students to name as many prehistoric animals as they can. This list goes well beyond that of dinosaurs, including woolly mammoths, giant sloths, and mastodons.

C. Ask students what tools paleontologists need to remove fossils from the ground.

D. Have students listen to the song "Let's Go on a Dinosaur Dig" to see if they listed all the tools mentioned in the song. The tools include camera, tape measure, jackhammer, geological hammer, brush, foil, tissue, plaster of Paris, magnifying glass, and rope.

E. Instruct students to create their own paleontology kits. Ask them to paint the exterior of the boxes they brought from home shades of brown. Allow the box to dry overnight before placing the tools in the kit.

F. Have students color and cut out the tools on the two **Paleontologist Tools** sheets. Hand out a small square of foil and rope to each student. Explain that paleontologists wrap bones in foil before packaging them, and that scientists use rope to move larger bones. Say the names of the tools aloud.

G. Ask students to answer the questions on **Tool Tasks** as a class. After each question, have students hold up the tool being discussed.

Closure
Ask students to draw themselves in their journals as paleontologists. They should be pictured using the tools required for this field of science. Under the picture have students complete this sentence:

I used my _____ to uncover _____.
           (tool name)   **(dinosaur or other ancient remains)**

Extension
Review what a paleontologist does by reading aloud *Digging up Dinosaurs*.

Assessment
Check the drawing and sentence for accuracy.

Paleontologist Tools

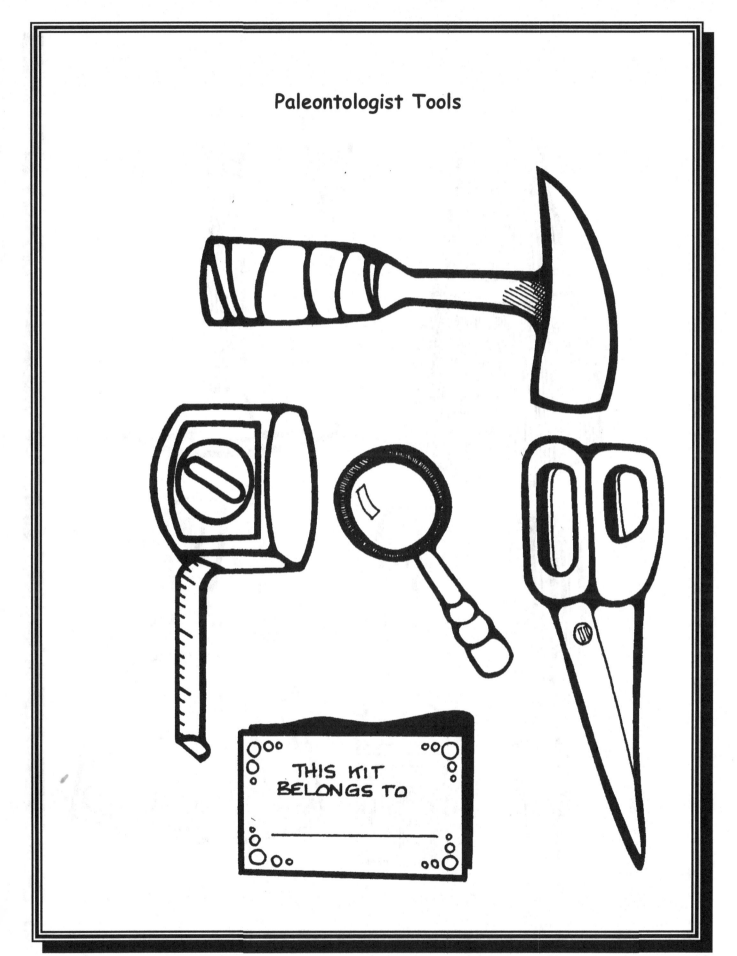

THIS KIT BELONGS TO

_____

Tool Tasks

Instructions

Read each question to the class. Ask students to hold up the tool that best fits the description.

1. Which tool has two sharp blades for cutting paper, fabric, or other items?
(Scissors)

2. Which hand-sized tool is used to brush or remove debris in a sweeping motion?
(Whiskbroom)

3. What tool has a glass lens that makes things look bigger?
(Magnifying lens)

4. Which tool is used to calculate the length between bones and fossil fragments in millimeters, centimeters, inches, or feet?
(Measuring tape)

5. What tool is used to break and remove rocks using a pointed end and a flat, thick end?
(Geological hammer)

6. Which tool has a flat, sharp edge that is used to shape wood, stone, or metal?
(Chisel)

7. What tool has pointed metal ends and is used for breaking up soil and rocks?
(Marsh pick)

8. What tool helps brush away dust and sand in small crevices?
(Paintbrush)

9. What item is used to wrap dinosaur bones before they are packaged?
(Foil)

10. What is used to package bones in a type of cast to keep them from breaking while they are shipped?
(Plaster of Paris; show some to the class)

11. Which tool scoops up debris so that it can be moved out of the way?
(Dustpan)

12. Which tool has a sharp point used for making holes in stone?
(Awl—pronounced "all")

Activity 42—Solving the Puzzle

Instructional Materials
- newspaper strips,
- glue or glue stick,
- scissors,
- paleontologist tools (cut-outs from previous activity),

Optional:
- bag of small shells,
- plaster of Paris,
- foil (large enough pieces to completely cover a shell),
- small paper cups (large enough to hold the shell),
- large mixing bowl or container,
- wooden spoon or craft sticks, and
- nonstick cooking spray.

Preparation
Place several books around the room showing prehistoric animals so students have an idea of the type of animal they are re-creating.

Decide which **Prehistoric Puzzle** sheet each pair will complete. Make copies of the puzzles, cut them apart, and put one piece of each puzzle aside.

Background Information
Some remains of **prehistoric** animals are called fossils. It is the scientist's job to try to put them back together. Scientists rarely find a complete dinosaur. The bones have been subject to many years of wear and tear. Some are broken or shattered. Others may have been dragged off years ago by scavengers or destroyed by insects. The conditions must be right to preserve a dinosaur. Some of the best and most complete finds have been dinosaurs that got trapped in tar pits or frozen in ice.

A. When students begin arriving, ask them to find their paleontologist kits and begin lining the inside of the box with newspaper. Have them use scissors to trim the newspaper to fit as needed. Instruct them to attach the paper using glue or a glue stick.

B. Have students place their paleontology tools inside their kits and design a nameplate to glue to the kits. Ask students to make sure their kits contain all the correct supplies.

C. Explain that when the bones of prehistoric animals are found they usually aren't easy to put together. It is very much like a puzzle with some pieces missing.

D. Have students work as partners to put together one of the **Prehistoric Puzzle** sheets (see Preparation). One puzzle is easier than the other. Explain that when paleontologists find bones of a fossil missing, they reconstruct what they think the missing part would look like. Tell students that they'll have to reconstruct the missing puzzle pieces, just like paleontologists do.

E. Have students glue the completed puzzles to construction paper and draw what they think the missing piece looks like. After students have completed their puzzle give them the missing puzzle piece to see how close they got to the original.

F. Ask students to evaluate the skills needed to excavate a dinosaur skeleton. Have partners look through the Scientist Skills Cards and determine which skills were most important. Discuss how they were used as a group.

EVALUATE!

G. Have students look though their paleontologist kits. Ask which tool they think they would have used the most had they really been uncovering the animal on the puzzle.

Closure
Have students identify the prehistoric animal they put together. (Tyrannosaurus rex or woolly mammoth).

Extensions
A. Have students complete the other puzzle.

B. Demonstrate how scientists protect bones for shipping. Follow the instructions on **Protecting the Bones** and have students pack their own fossils for shipping.

Assessment
Check to see if students reconstructed the missing pieces of the puzzle.

Prehistoric Puzzle 1

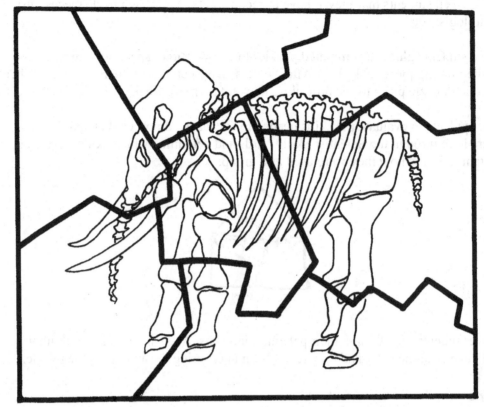

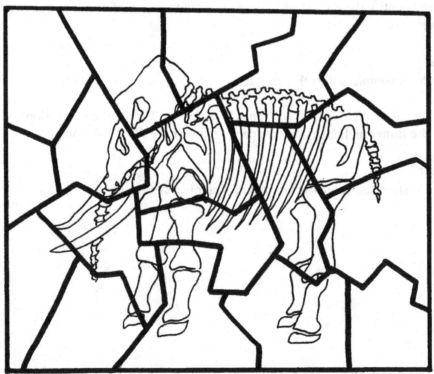

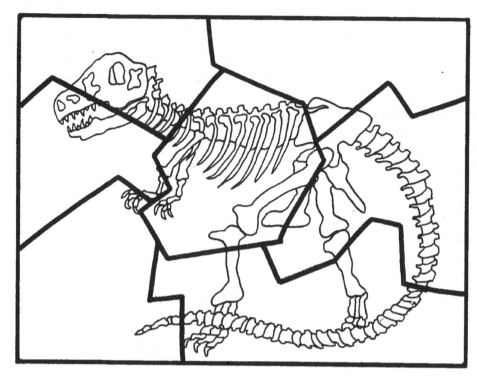

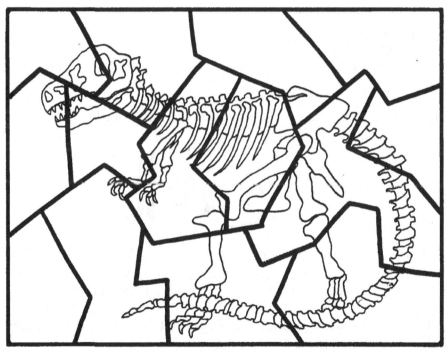

Protecting the Bones

Tell students to pretend to be scientists packing very important fossils to ship to a museum. This is how a paleontologist might package a bone to protect it on its journey.

Instructional Materials
- mixing bowl or plastic container,
- small bag of shells,
- large container of plaster of Paris,
- foil,
- 1 small paper cup per student,
- wooden spoon or craft sticks, and
- nonstick cooking spray

Instructions

1. Spray the inside of the plastic cups with nonstick cooking spray, then distribute the cups.

2. Give each student a seashell small enough to fit completely inside the cup. Provide small sheets of foil to wrap the shell.

3. Mix the plaster of Paris while students are covering the seashells with foil.

4. Fill each cup half full of plaster. Tell students to count to 50. When they finish counting, they can place their shells (which are covered in foil) in the plaster. Tell them to push the shells in gently so the bottom portion sinks into the plaster.

5. Cover the partially submerged shell with plaster. Fill the cup enough to cover the shell completely with plaster of Paris.

6. Let the plaster dry for several hours.

7. When the plaster has dried, have students peel off the paper cup. Explain that this is how paleontologists protect bones during shipment.

8. Allow students to take their plaster molds home. Tell them to work with a parent to remove the shell from the plaster.

Activity 43—Dino Discoveries

Instructional Materials
♦ student journals;
♦ *A Dinosaur Named Sue* by Fay Robinson;
♦ crayons or map pencils;

Optional:
♦ *Whatever Happened to the Dinosaurs?* and *Where to Look for a Dinosaur* books, both by Bernard Most; and
♦ *A Dinosaur Named After Me* book, by Bernard Most.

Preparation
Display dinosaur reference books around the classroom. Make an example of an illustration of yourself and a dinosaur to share with students.

Background Information
The word **dinosaur** comes from two Greek words. The word *deinos* means terrible, and the word *sauros* means lizard. The most famous terrible lizard was the tyrannosaurus, whose name means tyrant-lizard. A **tyrant** is someone who rules in a cruel and unjust way. Names given to dinosaurs usually have a story behind them. Some names describe how the animal behaved. Other names might tell about the dinosaur's physical traits or where it was discovered, and some were named after people.

A. Read aloud the book *A Dinosaur Named After Me* (if available). Tell students that it is an honor for a paleontologist to have the chance to name a newly discovered dinosaur. Explain that they will pretend to discover a new dinosaur today. They will have the honor, as do other paleontologists, of naming it after themselves.

B. Tell students they should select a dinosaur they have things in common with. For example: slow, fast, vegetarian, carnivore, tall, short, etc. Instruct students to draw this dinosaur with a few personal modifications.

C. Have students write the following in their journal:

The dinosaur I choose is _____.

_____ + _____ = _____
  (my name)   (dinosaur's name)   (new dinosaur's name)

Here's an example: Brenda + Spinosaurus = **Brendinosaurus**

Closure
Have students share their namesake dinosaurs. Have them explain what dinosaur they chose to modify and why.

Extensions
A. Read aloud *A Dinosaur Named Sue* and have students reenact her discovery.

B. Read aloud *Whatever Happened to the Dinosaurs?* and *Where to Look for a Dinosaur.*

C. Ask students which dinosaur has the longest name. It's the *micropachycephalosaurus*, which means small, thick-headed lizard.

Assessment
Assess the Closure activity.

Activity 44—Colorful Dinosaurs

Instructional Materials
- reference books about dinosaurs,
- *25 Fun Adventure Songs* CD or audiotape,
- paint,
- cotton swabs,
- sponge (cut into small squares for painting), and
- watercolors.

Preparation
Make several copies of **Dino Patterns** for the class. Set up stations for painting and designing dinosaurs.

Background Information
We'll never know what colors dinosaurs really were. Although we find fossilized skin, time does not fossilize color or markings. That means illustrations in books that show dinosaurs with stripes and colors really came from the imagination of a scientist or an author. All paleontologists have their own ideas of how they think dinosaurs looked. Some may have been camouflaged to protect themselves where they grazed or hunted. Others may have been brightly colored to ward off predators. Some scientists even think there were dinosaurs that changed colors at different times of the year.

A. Have students tell you what color they think dinosaurs were and why. (They probably think dinosaurs are the colors they see in books and on toys.)

B. Explain that it is impossible to know exactly what color dinosaurs were but that paleontologists use research and deductive reasoning to draw conclusions. (Share the Background Information.)

C. Ask students how they think animals living today could help paleontologists figure out what color dinosaurs might have been. (Male animals are usually brighter in color than females, many animals blend in to their surroundings, many animals have bright colors or markings to scare off predators, etc.)

D. Have students sing "What Colors Were the Dinosaurs?"

E. Ask students to pick a pattern from the **Dino Pattern** sheets. Ask students whether the dinosaur is an herbivore or a carnivore. Ask them to think about what colors would be best in each dinosaur's surroundings. After choosing colors, ask students to make their dinosaurs unique using options that you will write on the board.

F. Copy the below list of dinosaur patterns and instructions on how to make them. Then ask students what these names tell us about each dinosaur.

Dotasaurus—a dotted dinosaur made using a cotton swab
Stripasaurus—a dinosaur with a pattern of stripes
Washasaurus—a dinosaur made with a watercolor wash that blends together
Spongeasaurus—a dinosaur with a sponge pattern to its skin
Texturasaurus—a dinosaur placed over a surface of texture, which is rubbed over with crayon to create a unique pattern on the skin

G. Allow students to paint their dinosaurs, then display the artwork in the classroom.

Closure
Ask students the following discussion questions: Which colors are most common of animals that live today? What do animals use their color for? If you lived in the woods, what colors would you use to camouflage yourself?

Extensions
Create a dinosaur art museum, with labels, for the room or hallway.

Assessment
Check for reasoning skills that demonstrate the reasons for dinosaur coloring.

Dino Pattern—Stegasaurus

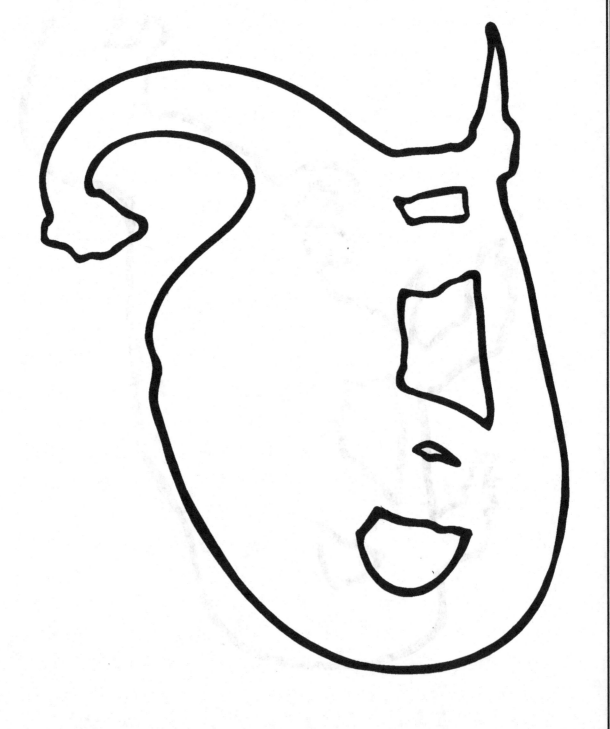

Activity 45—Missing?

Instructional Materials
- *What Happened to the Dinosaurs?* book, by Franklyn M. Branley;
- student journals;
- 1 Paleontology Badge per student;

Optional:
- newspaper (strips and whole pages);
- glue;
- water;
- small plastic containers;
- masking tape; and
- paint (black and white to mix for gray).

Preparation
Make a glue-and-water mixture to use as an adhesive. Collect several sheets of newspaper for each student. Cut strips of newspaper.

Background Information
No one knows exactly how the dinosaurs disappeared. There are many theories. The most popular theory is that a large asteroid crashed into Earth's surface millions of years ago. Scientists have discovered a large impact crater near the Yucatan Peninsula of Mexico. The crater hole is 124 miles across. This impact sent tons of debris into the atmosphere, blocking out much of the sun's heat and energy. Plants, then herbivores, and finally carnivorous dinosaurs died.

A. Read aloud *What Happened to the Dinosaurs?* Ask students what they think happened. Share the Background Information.

B. Play a game of Asteroid Tag. Ask for a volunteer to be an asteroid, then instruct the rest of the students to be dinosaurs. Set a boundary for play. When the asteroid tags a dinosaur, the dinosaur has to freeze. An extreme temperature change is what many scientists believed may have caused dinosaurs to die out. As players freeze, explain that this is what may have happened to the dinosaurs.

C. Have students look on a map of your state and use the legend to determine what would be 124 miles across. If an asteroid of this size hit your state, what area would it cover?

D. Ask students to find the Yucatan Peninsula of Mexico on a map.

E. Review the past five activities and ask students what they have learned about paleontology.

Closure
Close paleontology kits and congratulate students on completing their paleontology studies. Hand out Paleontology Badges and allow students to cut and paste the badges onto their diplomas.

Extension
Ask students to create a large asteroid using newspaper, papier-mâché, and the **Asteroid** sheet.

Assessment
Assess student understanding of the theory behind the extinction of the dinosaurs by asking the following questions:

♦ What would happen to the ground if an asteroid 124 miles across hit the Earth?
♦ Where would all the dirt and rocks go?
♦ What makes it possible for us to live on Earth and be warm?
♦ What would happen if we didn't receive light and energy from the sun?
♦ How might the dirt and rocks in the atmosphere affect sunlight on Earth?
♦ What effects might this have had on plants and animals?

Asteroid

Instructional Materials

- ◆ newspaper (strips and whole pages),
- ◆ glue,
- ◆ water,
- ◆ small plastic containers,
- ◆ masking tape, and
- ◆ paint (black and white to mix for gray).

Instructions

1. Crumple pieces of newspaper into a ball. Use masking tape to hold the ball together. Connect a large piece of tape running north to south and a piece of tape connecting east to west.

2. Using strips of newspaper and a papier-mâché mix, cover the ball and mold it into an asteroid.

3. Let the asteroid dry.

4. Paint it.

Activity 46—Lifting Dinosaurs

Instructional Materials
- shoe box lid or similar size box lid (with sides);
- books or old telephone books;
- newspaper;
- golf ball, marbles, old toy cars, or other items that will roll;
- paints (any color);
- art paper;
- 1 Physics Badge per student;

Optional Materials
- clay;
- cotton balls;
- paper clip;
- 2 small stickers; and
- *How Do You Lift a Lion?* book, by Robert E. Wells.

Preparation
Make a copy of the Physics Badge for each student. Find extra box lids, just in case.

Background Information
Physics is the study of how the world works. **Work**, in physics terms, is the amount of force used to complete a task. Scientists who study physics are interested in measurement, motion, light, gravity, time, mass, sound, and many other things.

Physics also includes the study of **simple machines**. Machines make work easier and faster. There are four simple machines that will be taught here: the lever, the pulley, the inclined plane, and the wheel and axle (gears and wedges are also considered simple machines.)**Force** is the push or pull exerted on an object. **Distance** refers to how far an object moves. The **load** is an object that is being lifted. A **fulcrum** is a point on which a lever rests or pivots.

A. Share the following dialogue: How would a paleontologist lift fossilized bones to get them into the museum? The bones may weigh 2,000 pounds. It would take many people to lift something this heavy. It's too impractical. Humans discovered this hundreds of years ago, so they invented simple machines to make work easier. (Share the Background Information.)

B. Introduce the Physics Badge. Tell students that they can work on completing the badge when they have free time between activities.

C. Ask students to brainstorm ways workers could get the bones into a museum. Brainstorm until someone comes up with the idea of using a ramp. This is a type of simple machine called an inclined plane. Discuss how the inclined plane would be used. (The dinosaur bones would be placed on a platform with wheels and rolled up a ramp.) Point out that the wheel and axle is another type of simple machine which will be discussed later.

D. Locate an inclined plane. There's probably one near an exit or an entrance to the school. Discuss the purpose of the inclined planes in your building. (special needs, delivering supplies, etc.)

E. Use an inclined plane in your building to show how simple machines can make work easier. Have students practice lifting a friend up the height of an inclined plane. Then have students push one another up the inclined plane in a rolling chair. Ask them which was easier. The inclined plane made the job easier.

F. Divide into lab groups. Have Chief Scientists gather supplies to complete the art project on **I Feel Inclined to Paint**. Have each student create a painting using an inclined plane or have each group create one piece and let everyone roll an object. Display art projects around the classroom and have students clean up work stations.

Closure
Hand out journals and ask student to draw a picture showing how an inclined plane can make work easier. Ask students to copy and complete the following sentences at the bottom of the page:

Inclined planes are simple machines. They help _____.

Extensions
A. Have students make a maze of inclined planes following the instructions on **A-Maze of Inclined Planes.**

B. Read aloud *How Do You Lift a Lion?* Then ask students to create a chart about the different kinds of simple machines. Have them list examples of each.

Assessment
Evaluate the journal entry for understanding of inclined planes.

I Feel Inclined to Paint

Instructional Materials

- shoe box lid or larger box lid (with sides);
- books or old telephone books;
- newspaper;
- golf ball, marbles, old toy cars, or other items that will roll; and
- paints (any color).

Instructions

1. Put newspaper down to protect the table.

2. Place a piece of art paper inside a shoe box lid or a larger box lid.

3. Place the lid on a flat surface and prop up one side using large books. (Old phone books work great.)

4. Dip a variety of round and rolling objects in any color paint and roll them down the inclined plane.

5. Display the finished "inclined designs" in the classroom.

A-Maze of Inclined Planes

Instructional Materials
- ♦ clay,
- ♦ shoe box or shoe box lid,
- ♦ marbles,
- ♦ cotton,
- ♦ paper clip, and
- ♦ 2 small stickers.

Instructions

1. Roll clay into long, thin strips. The number of strips needed depends on the difficulty of the maze students are about to create.

2. Use the strips of clay to create a maze, or labyrinth, inside the shoe box or shoe box lid. Make sure the aisles are large enough for a marble to roll through. Create a starting point in one corner of the box. Have the end of the maze in an opposite corner. Make angles, corners, and turns, and dead ends throughout the maze.

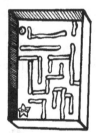

3. Use small stickers to show the starting point and the end.

4. Place a marble at the starting point. Hold the maze and tilt the inclined plane to move the marble through the aisles of the maze. Practice manipulating the inclined plane to roll the marble to the end.

5. Try moving a paper clip through the maze. Does it move easily on the inclined plane? What about a cotton ball? Can you think of another object that might work easily?

Activity 47—As Strong as a Lever

Instructional Materials
♦ 3 plastic cups,
♦ tape,
♦ 3 large markers,
♦ 3 rulers,
♦ 60 pennies or counting cubes,
♦ rulers to use as levers,
♦ large markers to use as fulcrums,
Optional:
♦ 1" x 4" piece of wood about 4 feet long, and
♦ a small, pointed piece of wood for the fulcrum.

Preparation
Test the Super Teacher activity before showing it to the class.

Background Information
A lever is one of the most commonly used simple machines. In fact, we have two built-in levers on our bodies. (Our arms.) A **lever** consists of a bar or plank that rotates on a **pivot point**. The pivot point is called the **fulcrum**. The **load** is the object being supported. A seesaw is one type of lever. It is called a first-class lever. A first class lever has the fulcrum between the force and load arms.

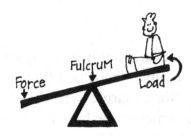

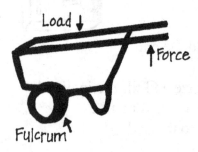

Another type of lever is a wheel barrow. This is a second-class lever. A second-class lever has the fulcrum on one end with the load in the middle and force arm on the other end.

Your arm is a lever. The pivot point is your elbow, the force is your hand, and the load is what goes in you hand.

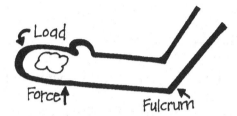

A. Review the previous discussion about simple machines. Ask the question: What type of simple machine is a seesaw? (Share the Background Information.) Discuss the different locations of the fulcrum, force, and load on the three different levers.

B. Divide into lab groups. Give each Chief Scientist a ruler, a marker, and a heavy book. Ask groups to determine how they can lift the book off the table or floor without touching it with their hands. After several minutes explain that if they put the marker under the ruler (Like a seesaw) and used the ruler to lift the book they just created a first-class lever. This is one of the simplest ways to lift heavy objects with very little effort.

C. Ask each Chief Scientist to tape a cup to the center of the table for the next experiment.

D. Instruct students to use their marker and ruler as a first-class lever as they put a penny on the load arm of the lever and attempt to flip the coin into the cup. Demonstrate how to use the lever before students try. Instruct students to be careful, and make sure no students sit where they could get hit by pennies.

E. Before they begin, have students estimate the number of coins they will flip into their cups (out of 25 tries).

F. Encourage students to adjust the length of the load and effort arms (ruler), as well as the distance of the lever from the cup.

G. Have students draw this illustration in their journals. Have them label the page First-Class Lever and label the marker as a **fulcrum** and the ruler as a **lever**.

Closure

Discuss what students learned about how the position of the lever on the fulcrum affected the flip. For example: The closer the fulcrum was to the penny.

Extensions

A. Have students graph their estimates then their actual results.

B. Ask students to find a seesaw and experiment with different weights on each side.

C. Perform the optional activity on **Super Teacher** if you have the materials. Remind student not to try this activity at home. This lab should only be performed by an adult.

Assessment

Check for understanding during the Closure discussion.

Instructional Materials
♦ 1" x 4" piece of wood about 4 feet long; and
♦ a small, pointed piece of wood for the fulcrum.

Instructions
1. Park your car on a flat surface and set the parking break.

2. Put the lever (board) under one of your tires.

3. Place the fulcrum (small piece of wood) as close to the car (load) as you can. Remind students that the closer you place the fulcrum to the load when using a first-class lever, the less work is necessary to do the job.

4. Once the fulcrum and the lever are in place, gently push downward on the board and your car will lift off the ground.

5. Remind students they should never try to perform this lab without an adult.

Activity 48—A Wave of Sounds

Instructional Materials
- *25 Fun Adventure Songs* CD or audiotape,
- 6 empty tin cans,
- 1 nail,
- 1 hammer,
- radio,
- several grains of rice or dry cereal, and

Optional:
- whale songs on CD or tape.

Preparation
Use the hammer and nail to make a small hole in the bottom of each can. Make sure the hole is in the center of each can.

Background Information
Physics includes the study of **matter**. Matter is anything that has weight and takes up space, such as a solid, liquid, or gas. A person who specializes in physics is called a physicist. Physics explains a variety of things in our world, such as why a seesaw works, how hot air rises, and how sounds waves travel. Physics explains how electricity works, how magnets attract, and how light travels in waves.

Sound is an energy form that travels in waves. Sound occurs when an object **vibrates** rapidly. When the back-and-forth motion of vibration stops, the sound stops. When we talk, the air in our lungs pushes up and vibrates our vocal cords. The more rapid the vibrations, the higher the pitch (or sound). The slower the vibrations, the lower the sound. **Pitch** is the sound quality referring to the highness or lowness of a tone.

A. Begin by speaking without letting any sound come from your mouth. Then tell students that you stopped your voice box from vibrating, and that's why no sound came out.

B. Ask students if they know what causes sound. (Vibrations.) Share the Background Information. Share the optional **Rubber Band Guitar** activity to demonstrate different sounds at different vibrations. (Only the teacher may set up this activity.)

C. Have students feel their vocal cords in their necks. Ask them to make a low-pitched sound and feel the vibrations in their voice boxes. Then ask them to make a high-pitched sound and feel the vibrations. Ask them if they felt the difference.

D. Sound travels in waves, like the transfer of energy in the waves of the ocean. Ask students whether these waves can travel through solid, liquid, or gaseous substances. Then ask the following questions:

◆ Can you hear sounds underwater?
◆ Can you hear someone talking through a wall?
◆ Can you hear sounds in the air?

E. Demonstrate that you can feel and see evidence of sound waves. Turn on a radio and turn up the volume. Position the radio so the speakers are directed toward the ceiling. Put a piece of paper over one of the speakers. Pour the rice or cereal on the paper and observe the rice or cereal.

F. Play "Can You Name These Sounds?" from the CD or audiotape and have students sing along.

G. Have each lab group make a telephone following the instructions on **Tin Can Telephone** to demonstrate how sound waves travel through solid substances.

H. Ask students to lie on their backs with their arms at their sides and their eyes closed. Tell them to pretend they're in a bathtub, lying back in the water, with their ears submerged but their faces out of the water. Ask what they hear if they tap their fingernails on the bottom of the tub. Ask the following: What do you hear as you inhale? What if you start singing? (Determine that sound can travel through water.)

I. Ask students how sound travels through a gas. See if they can figure it out!

Closure
Distribute journals and ask students to illustrate how sound travels though solid, liquid, and gaseous substances.

Extensions
A. Listen to whale songs to demonstrate how animal sounds can travel through the ocean.

B. Have students draw pictures in their journals showing a woman screaming after seeing a mouse. Ask students to show the sound waves traveling in all directions. If the scream is high-pitched, the sound waves should be fast (closer together).

Assessment
Check journal entries for understanding.

Rubber Band Guitar

Instructional Materials
- small piece of wood,
- nails,
- hammer, and
- rubber bands of equal length.

Instructions

1. Hammer the nails into a small piece of wood.

2. Attach rubber bands to each nail set. The rubber bands will stretch different distances.

3. Strum the rubber bands and listen to the different sounds. The rubber bands that are stretched the farthest will have a quicker vibration when strummed. This will create a higher pitch.

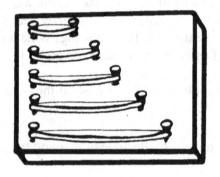

Tin Can Telephones

Instructional Materials
♦ 2 empty tin cans (each with a hole in the bottom) per lab group,
♦ 1 ruler, and
♦ string.

Instructions

1. Use a ruler to measure 10 feet of string. Thread one end of the string through the hole in one can. Tie a large knot in that end of the string so it can't slip through the hole. Repeat with the other end of the string and the other can.

2. Two people hold a can and stand apart so the string is stretched tightly. Take turns talking into the cans and listening.

3. Now stretch the string around a corner and talk on your tin can telephones again. What happens?

4. Ask another student to stand between your tin can telephones and pinch the string while you try to talk and listen. What happens?

Activity 49—Albert Einstein

Instructional Materials
♦ scissors;
♦ marker, crayons, or map pencils; and
♦ a stapler.

Preparation
Make 1 copy of **Albert Einstein's Story** for each student.

A. Tell students that Albert Einstein, the most well-known **physicist** in the world, was born in 1879 and died in 1955. Ask students to calculate how long Einstein lived.

B. Read the Einstein story with the class in unison.

C. Have students finish the drawing on the last page of the book. Color the illustrations.

D. Have partners take turns reading the book to each other.

Closure
Have students share their drawings with a partner. Congratulate students on completing their physics studies. Have them color, cut, and glue their Physics Badges to their diplomas.

Extension
Share an age-appropriate biography about Albert Einstein. Two suggestions are *Albert Einstein* by Ibi Lepscky, or *Albert Einstein: Young Thinker* by Marie Hammontree.

Assessment
Ask the following comprehension questions to assess understanding. What kind of scientist was Einstein? What award did he win? What was Einstein like as a child?

Albert Einstein's Story

Albert Einstein was a curious little boy. He was always trying to figure out how things worked. He was always trying to figure out why things worked.

When he was young, Albert didn't do well in school. He was very smart but daydreamed a lot in class.

He was always figuring out hard math problems, which helped him find answers to science problems.

He called one of his ideas an electric eye. This idea made the invention of television possible.

One of his ideas was so good that he got the greatest award a scientist can receive. He won the Nobel Prize for physics.

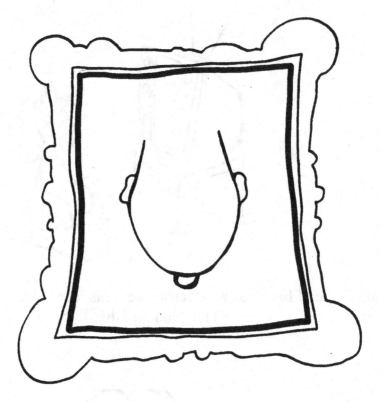

Many people say Albert Einstein was the smartest person in the world. Draw a picture of the person you think is the smartest in the world.

Activity 50—Graduation Day

Instructional Materials
- student journals,
- snacks,
- drinks,
- paper plates,
- napkins,

Optional:
- 1 grocery sack per student,
- white paint, and
- a black marker.

Preparation
If desired, complete Lab Jacket. Bring snacks and drinks for after-ceremony refreshments. Sign each diploma and place a sticker on each one.

A. Congratulate students for making it to the end of an exciting science journey. Compliment students on how hard they worked. Give them their completed diplomas with all badges attached.

B. Ask students if they can remember all the sciences they studied to earn their Ph.D. badges.

C. Ask the following questions:
- How did chemistry connect to entomology?
- How did entomology connect to meteorology?
- How did meteorology connect to astronomy?
- How did astronomy connect to oceanography?
- How did oceanography connect to zoology?
- How did zoology connect to physics?

D. Lay out the Scientist Skills Cards on the desk. Ask for volunteers to share how scientists use the skills and how they used them throughout the unit.

E. Have a small graduation ceremony. Invite each student to the front, one at a time, complimenting them on their hard work. Try to individualize for each student by citing something each did well. You could even place an official Ph.D. jacket on each student.

F. Ask students to pick one of their favorite games played during Ph.D., then take the class outside to play.

Closure
Thank everyone for participating. Distribute science journals and completed activities for students to take home. Sing "I'm a Scientist" one last time.

Ph.D. Jacket

Instructional Materials
- ◆ 1 paper grocery sack per student,
- ◆ white paint,
- ◆ scissors, and
- ◆ a black marker.

Instructions

1. Turn a paper sack into a jacket. Begin by cutting out the neck area of the jacket. Note the illustration below.

2. Cut out arm holes.

3. Paint the jacket white like a lab coat.

4. Write Dr. _____ Ph.D. on each coat.

(student's name)

5. Present the coats at the graduation ceremony.

Diploma

Badges

Name _____

Ph.D.—Doctor of Sciences
Materials Checklist

Note: Paper and pencils should be on-hand each day, as should art supplies including tape, scissors, and stapler, and may not be listed on the Checklist.

Activity	Vocabulary	Materials Needed
1	hypothesis	*25 Fun Adventure Songs* CD or Audiotape ½ cup vinegar ½ cup water 2 tablespoons baking soda 2 hard-boiled eggs 2 paper or plastic cups (with lids if possible)
2	science	*What Is a Scientist?* book by Barbara Lehn 1 envelope per student or make construction paper envelopes
3	sorting classify characteristics cooperation	***What Is a Scientist?* book** *25 Fun Adventure Songs* CD or audiotape *
4	circumference continents countries chemical reaction	*What Is a Scientist?* book 1 package of dry yeast ½ cup sugar 1 empty water bottle timer or stopwatch balloon (that fits over top of water bottle) poster board or butcher paper world map or atlas globe
5		3 Test Tube Adventures kits from the Wild Goose Company* variety of screw-on plastic lids and caps 2-liter soda bottle
6	entomologist oceanographer meteorologist astronomer chemist physicist zoologist paleontologist	
7	chemistry	*25 Fun Adventure Songs* CD or audiotape* 2 clumps of steel wool oil 2 flat containers to hold liquids 2 craft sticks permanent marker

		Optional: yarn or pipe cleaners for arms and legs
8	disproving carbon dioxide	3 Test Tube Adventures kits *25 Fun Adventure Songs* CD or audiotape **Optional:** A-1 Steak Sauce penny
9		3 Test Tube Adventures kits
10		3 Test Tube Adventures kits
11	polystyrene	3 Test Tube Adventures kits **Optional:** computer with Internet access
12	agriculture	*A Weed Is a Flower* book by Aliki **Optional:** bag of peanuts computer with Internet access
13	exoskeleton invertebrate thorax abdomen antennae entomologists	age-appropriate insect reference books *25 Fun Adventure Songs* CD or audiotape 1 paper bag per lab group 1 die per lab group **Optional:** *Insects Are My Life* book, by Megan McDonald
14	camouflage mimicry predators protection characteristics	insect research books brown sticks from outdoors 3 brown pipe cleaners per student 1 insect field guide per lab group self-adhesive notes **Optional:** *Bugs For Lunch* book, by Margery Facklam computer with Internet access
15	catapulting	age-appropriate insect research books string yardsticks or tape measures plastic test tubes from Test Tube Adventures kits tissue or paper towels to stop up the ends of test tubes **Optional:** 1 large milk carton per lab group panty hose (cut the toe so it can cover a milk carton)
16	migratory vegetation	paper clips (1 inch) tape measures or rulers string
17	simple eyes compound eyes image	1 egg carton per 6 students pipe cleaners straws **Optional:** *Charlotte's Web* book by E.B. White

		computer with Internet access
18	social insects communicate community	*25 Fun Adventure Songs* CD or audiotape *One Hundred Hungry Ants* book, by Elinor J. Pinczes black construction paper
19	arthropods arachnids hourglass	nylon rope or a full ball of yarn stakes to place in the ground black and brown construction paper 8 pipe cleaners per student (brown or black cut into equal sizes) white paint marble deep baking pan
20	predicting meteorology forecasting Fahrenheit Celsius	2 weather thermometers construction paper (large manila and red)
21	front folklore symbol	25 *Fun Adventure Songs* CD or audiotape* *Cloudy With a Chance of Meatballs* book, by Judi Barrett yarn (red and blue) **Optional:** recorded weather report from a local newspaper
22	evaporation dew water vapor	5 heavy-duty pipe cleaners per student (4 white, 1 blue) 1 sheet of light blue tissue paper per student yarn **Optional:** ice hot tap water metal cake pan wide-mouth glass jar
23	cumulus cumulonimbus cirrus stratus onomatopoeia	*The Cloud Book* by Tomi De Paolo *25 Fun Adventure Songs* CD or audiotape* newspaper or gray tissue paper **Optional:** *Thunder Cake* book, by Patricia Polacco gray paint *Thunder Cake* recipe supplies
24	season	
25	astronomy	books about the solar system **Optional:** computer with Internet access
26	stars constellation black dwarf black hole	**Optional:** audiotape of classical music

27	energy asteroid sundial	*25 Fun Adventure Songs* CD or audiotape* *Why the Sun and the Moon Live in the Sky* book, by Elphinstone Dayrell *Anansi the Spider* book, by Gerald McDermott
28	gravity	bubble liquid and wands **Optional:** *Astronaut: Living in Space* book, by Kate Hayden
29	galaxies	large sheet of butcher paper (preferably white)
30	oceanography low tide high tide tide pools	books about the ocean 1 wire hanger per student yarn (blue or black) **Optional:** *Life in a Tide Pool* book, by Allan Fowler ocean sounds CD or audiotape seashell collection computer with Internet access
31	Atlantic Pacific Arctic Indian sea	globe or a large world map **Optional:** recycled items, scraps (see the Extension activity)
32	trough crest currents wave wavelength	clear glass baking dish plastic test tubes from Test Tube Adventures kits blue food coloring baby oil **Optional:** ocean sounds on CD or audiotape
33	aqualung oceanographer	references about Jacques Cousteau **Optional:** computer with Internet access
34	sunlight zone twilight zone abyssal zone	ocean reference books butcher paper (3 rectangular pieces of equal size: 1 light blue, 1 dark blue, 1 black) tempera paint Optional: computer with Internet access
35	blubber baleen	reference books about whales tape measures or yardsticks *25 Fun Adventure Songs* CD or audiotape* Large, clear measuring cup oatmeal, small pasta, granola (or other small material to pass through a strainer) strainer
36	zoology reptiles amphibians	*25 Fun Adventure Songs* CD or audiotape* *Baby Whales Drink Milk* book, by Barbara Juster Esbensen

	classification	**Optional:** *Tuesday* book, by David Wiesner
37	fact opinion body language observation	**Optional:** CD or audiotape of animal sounds
38	verses patterns	**Optional:** *Animal Tracks* book, by Arthur Durros
39	research	**library books and assorted references on animals** old socks paper bags double-sided mounting tape scrap felt or art foam yarn (assorted colors) miscellaneous recycled items or craft supplies (for puppet making)
40	enormous	**Optional:** bathroom scale calculator
41	paleontology fossils geology extinct	*25 Fun Adventure Songs* CD or audiotape paint (shades of brown) paintbrushes **Optional:** aluminum foil (small square per student) (1) 5-inch piece of rope per student *Dinosaur's Day* book, by Ruth Thomson *Dinosaur World* book, by Christopher Santoro; *Dinosaurs Are Different* book, by Aliki *Digging up Dinosaurs* book, by Aliki
42	prehistoric	newspaper strips paleontologist tools (cut-outs from previous activity) **Optional Materials:** bag of small shells plaster of Paris foil (large enough pieces to completely cover a shell) small paper cups (large enough to hold the shell) large mixing bowl or container wooden spoon or craft sticks nonstick cooking spray
43	dinosaurs tyrant	*A Dinosaur Named Sue by Fay Robinson* **Optional:** *A Dinosaur Named After Me book,* by Bernard Most *Whatever Happened to the Dinosaurs?* and *Where to Look for a Dinosaur* books, both by Bernard Most
44	camouflage predators	reference books about dinosaurs *25 Fun Adventure Songs* CD or audiotape

	prey	paint cotton swabs sponge (cut into small squares for painting) watercolors
45	asteroid	*What Happened to the Dinosaurs?* book, by Franklyn M. Branley **Optional:** newspaper (strips and whole pages) small plastic containers paint (black and white to mix for gray)
46	physics work simple machines force load distance fulcrum	shoe box lid or similar size box lid (with sides) books or old telephone books newspaper golf ball, marbles, old toy cars, or other items that will roll paints (any color) **Optional:** clay cotton balls paper clip 2 small stickers *How Do You Lift a Lion?* book, by Robert E. Wells
47	lever pivot point load fulcrum	3 plastic cups 3 rulers 60 pennies or counting cubes rulers to use as levers large markers to use as fulcrums **Optional:** 1" x 4" piece of wood about 4 feet long small, pointed piece of wood for the fulcrum
48	matter sound vibrates pitch	*25 Fun Adventure Songs* CD or audiotape* 6 empty tin cans 1 nail 1 hammer radio several grains of rice or dry cereal **Optional:** whale songs on CD or audiotape
49	physicist	
50	graduation diploma	refreshments paper plates napkins **Optional:** 1 grocery sack per student white paint

Ph.D.—Doctor of Sciences

TEKS Checklist

Activity	TEKS: Language Arts and Reading	TEKS: Mathematics	TEKS: Social Studies	TEKS: Science
1	Write to record ideas and reflections Record knowledge of a topic in various ways, such as by drawing pictures, making lists, and showing connections among ideas Connect experiences and ideas with those of others through speaking and listening		Communicate in written, oral, and visual forms Identify characteristics and qualities of careers in science	Plan and conduct simple descriptive investigations Construct reasonable explanations and draw conclusions using information Explain the problem in his or her own words and identify a task and solution related to the task

Activity	TEKS: Language Arts and Reading	TEKS: Mathematics	TEKS: Social Studies	TEKS: Science
2	Ask and answer relevant questions and make contributions in small- or large-group discussions Connect experiences and ideas with those of others through speaking and listening Decode by using all letter-sound correspondence within a word Discuss meanings of words and develop vocabulary through meaningful and concrete experiences Record knowledge of a topic in various ways, such as by drawing pictures, making lists, and showing connections among ideas Listen responsively to stories and other texts read aloud, including selections from classic and contemporary works		Communicate in written, oral, and visual forms Identify characteristics and qualities of careers in science	Construct reasonable explanations and draw conclusions using information and prior knowledge Communicate explanations about investigations
3	Determine the purposes for listening, such as to get information, to solve problems, and to enjoy and appreciate Connect experiences and ideas with those of others through speaking and listening Discuss meanings of words and develop vocabulary through meaningful or concrete experiences Ask and answer relevant questions and make contributions in small- or large-group discussions	Select or develop an appropriate problem-solving strategy, including drawing a picture, looking for a pattern, systematic guessing and checking, or acting out Use attributes to describe how two shapes or solids are alike or different Describe and identify objects in order to sort them according to a given attribute using informal language Reason and support his or her thinking using objects, words,	Communicate in written, oral, and visual forms Identify characteristics and qualities of careers in science	

Activity	TEKS: Language Arts and Reading	TEKS: Mathematics	TEKS: Social Studies	TEKS: Science
	Draw conclusions from information gathered Write to record ideas and reflections	pictures, numbers, and technology Measure length, capacity, and weight using concrete models that approximate standard units		
4	Participate in rhymes, songs, conversations, and discussions Retell a spoken message by summarizing or clarifying Discuss meanings of words and develop vocabulary through meaningful and concrete experiences	Use organized data to construct real object graphs Estimate and measure circumference	Create and use simple maps to identify the location of places Create written and visual materials to express ideas	Observe, measure, predict, and record changes Develop ability necessary to do scientific inquiry in the field and the classroom Make decisions using information
5	Determine the purposes for listening, such as to get information, to solve problems, and to enjoy and appreciate Connect experiences and ideas with those of others through speaking and listening Write to record ideas and reflections Record knowledge of a topic in various ways, such as by drawing pictures, making lists, and showing connections among ideas		Communicate in written, oral, and visual forms Identify characteristics and qualities of careers in science	Construct reasonable explanations and draw conclusions using information and prior knowledge Communicate explanations about investigations Make decisions using information
6	Discuss meanings of words and develop vocabulary through meaningful and concrete experiences Use knowledge of word order (syntax) and context to support word identification and confirm meaning	Draw conclusions and answer questions based on picture graphs and bar-type graphs Use a problem-solving model that incorporates understanding the problem, making a plan, carrying out the plan, and evaluating the solution for	Identify characteristics and qualities of careers in science Express ideas orally, based on knowledge and experiences	

Activity	TEKS: Language Arts and Reading	TEKS: Mathematics	TEKS: Social Studies	TEKS: Science
	Use structural cues such as prefixes and suffixes to recognize words Record knowledge of a topic in various ways, such as by drawing pictures, making lists, and showing connections among ideas	reasonableness		
7	Determine the purposes for listening, such as to get information, to solve problems, and to enjoy and appreciate Connect experiences and ideas with those of others through speaking and listening Discuss meanings of words and develop vocabulary through meaningful and concrete experiences Ask and answer relevant questions and make contributions in small- or large-group discussions Record knowledge of a topic in various ways, such as by drawing pictures, making lists, and showing connections among ideas		Communicate in written, oral, and visual forms Identify characteristics and qualities of careers in science	Observe, measure, record, analyze, predict, and illustrate changes in size, mass, temperature, color, position, quantity, sound, and movement Plan and conduct simple descriptive investigations Gather information using simple equipment and tools to extend the senses Construct reasonable explanations and draw conclusions using information and prior knowledge Communicate explanations about investigations Demonstrate safe practices during classroom and field investigations
8	**Learn to apply letter-sound correspondences of a set of consonants and vowels to begin to read** Discuss meanings of words and develop vocabulary through meaningful and concrete experiences	Recognize that there are quantities less than a whole	Identify characteristics and qualities of careers in science Express ideas orally, based on knowledge and experiences	Demonstrate safe practices during classroom investigations Communicate explanations about investigations

Activity	TEKS: Language Arts and Reading	TEKS: Mathematics	TEKS: Social Studies	TEKS: Science
	Identify multisyllabic words by using common syllable patterns			
9	Ask and answer relevant questions and make contributions in small- or large-group discussions Record knowledge of a topic in various ways, such as by drawing pictures, making lists, and showing connections among ideas Read to accomplish various purposes, both assigned and self-selected		Identify characteristics and qualities of careers in science Communicate in written, oral, and visual forms	Demonstrate safe practices during classroom and field investigations Observe, measure, record, analyze, predict, and illustrate changes in size, mass, temperature, color, position, quantity, sound, and movement Plan and conduct simple descriptive investigations Gather information using simple equipment and tools to extend the senses Construct reasonable explanations and draw conclusions using information and prior knowledge Communicate explanations about investigations
10	Ask and answer relevant questions and make contributions in small- or large-group discussions Record knowledge of a topic in various ways, such as by drawing pictures, making lists, and showing connections among ideas Read to accomplish various purposes, both assigned and self-selected	Name fractional parts of a whole object when giving a concrete representation Use a problem-solving model that incorporates understanding the problem, making a plan, carrying out the plan, and evaluating for reasonableness Explain and record observations using objects, words, pictures, numbers, and technology	Identify characteristics and qualities of careers in science Communicate in written, oral, and visual forms	Demonstrate safe practices during classroom and field investigations Observe, measure, record, analyze, predict, and illustrate changes in size, mass, temperature, color, position, quantity, sound, and movement Plan and conduct simple descriptive investigations Gather information using simple equipment and tools to extend the senses Construct reasonable explanations and draw conclusions using

Activity	TEKS: Language Arts and Reading	TEKS: Mathematics	TEKS: Social Studies	TEKS: Science
				information and prior knowledge Communicate explanations about investigations
11	Ask and answer relevant questions and make contributions in small- or large-group discussions Record knowledge of a topic in various ways, such as by drawing pictures, making lists, and showing connections among ideas Read to accomplish various purposes, both assigned and self-selected	Name fractional parts of a whole object when giving a concrete representation Explain and record observations using objects, words, pictures, numbers, and technology	Identify characteristics and qualities of careers in science Communicate in written, oral, and visual forms	Demonstrate safe practices during classroom and field investigations Observe, measure, record, analyze, predict, and illustrate changes in size, mass, temperature, color, position, quantity, sound, and movement Plan and conduct simple descriptive investigations Gather information using simple equipment and tools to extend the senses Construct reasonable explanations and draw conclusions using information and prior knowledge Communicate explanations about investigations
12	Determine the purposes for listening, such as to get information, to solve problems, and to enjoy and appreciate Connect experiences and ideas with those of others through speaking and listening Draw conclusions from information gathered	Name fractional parts of a whole object when giving a concrete representation	Identify characteristics and qualities of careers in science Communicate in written, oral, and visual forms Identify historic figures, such as Henrietta King and Thurgood Marshall, who have influenced the community, state, and nation Explain how science and technology have changed the ways people meet basic needs	Demonstrate safe practices during classroom and field investigations Observe, measure, record, analyze, predict, and illustrate changes in size, mass, temperature, color, position, quantity, sound, and movement Plan and conduct simple descriptive investigations

Activity	TEKS: Language Arts and Reading	TEKS: Mathematics	TEKS: Social Studies	TEKS: Science
13	Connect experiences and ideas with those of others through speaking and listening Respond appropriately and courteously to directions and questions Discuss meanings of words and develop vocabulary through meaningful and concrete experiences Participate in rhymes, songs, conversations, and discussions Write to record ideas and reflections Record knowledge of a topic in various ways, such as by drawing pictures, making lists, and showing connections among ideas	Collect and sort data Use organized data to construct real object graphs, picture graphs, and bar-type graphs	Identify characteristics and qualities of careers in science Identify historic figures such as Amelia Earhart and Robert Fulton who have exhibited a love of individualism and inventiveness Express ideas orally based on knowledge and experiences	Make decisions using information Observe and describe the parts of plants and animals Identify characteristics of living organisms that allow their basic needs to be met

Activity	TEKS: Language Arts and Reading	TEKS: Mathematics	TEKS: Social Studies	TEKS: Science
14	Connect experiences and ideas with those of others through speaking and listening Respond appropriately and courteously to directions and questions Discuss meanings of words and develop vocabulary through meaningful and concrete experiences Record knowledge of a topic in various ways, such as by drawing pictures, making lists, and showing connections among ideas Read to accomplish various purposes, both assigned and self-selected Decode by using all letter-sound correspondences within a word			Make decisions using information Observe and describe the parts of plants and animals Identify characteristics of living organisms Compare and give examples of the ways living organisms depend on each other and their environments Identify characteristics of living organisms that allow their basic needs to be met

Activity	TEKS: Language Arts and Reading	TEKS: Mathematics	TEKS: Social Studies	TEKS: Science
15	Respond appropriately and courteously to directions and questions Discuss meanings of words and develop vocabulary through meaningful and concrete experiences Write to record ideas and reflections Record knowledge of a topic in various ways, such as by drawing pictures, making lists, and showing connections among ideas Write in different forms for different purposes, such as lists to record, letters to invite or thank, and stories or poems to entertain	Measure length, capacity, and weight using concrete models that approximate standard units	Identify characteristics and qualities of careers in science Express ideas orally based on knowledge and experiences	Observe and describe the parts of plants and animals Identify characteristics of living organisms Identify characteristics of living organisms that allow their basic needs to be met

Activity	TEKS: Language Arts and Reading	TEKS: Mathematics	TEKS: Social Studies	TEKS: Science
16	Respond appropriately and courteously to directions and questions Record knowledge of a topic in various ways, such as by drawing pictures, making lists, and showing connections among ideas Determine the purposes for listening, such as to get information, to solve problems, and to enjoy and appreciate	Use a problem-solving model that incorporates understanding the problem, making a plan, carrying out the plan, and evaluating the solution for reasonableness Measure length, capacity, and weight using concrete models that approximate standard units Recall and apply basic addition facts Model, create, and describe division situations in which a set of concrete objects is separated into equivalent sets Relate informal language to mathematical language and symbols		Observe and record the functions of animal parts Observe, measure, record, analyze, predict, and illustrate changes in size, mass, temperature, color, position, quantity, sound, and movement

Activity	TEKS: Language Arts and Reading	TEKS: Mathematics	TEKS: Social Studies	TEKS: Science
17	Determine the purposes for listening, such as to get information, to solve problems, and to enjoy and appreciate Record knowledge of a topic in various ways, such as by drawing pictures, making lists, and showing connections among ideas Respond appropriately and courteously to directions and questions Discuss meanings of words and develop vocabulary through meaningful and concrete experiences			Observe and describe the parts of plants and animals Identify characteristics of living organisms Identify characteristics of living organisms that allow their basic needs to be met
18	Participate in rhymes, songs, conversations, and discussions Determine the purposes for listening, such as to get information, to solve problems, and to enjoy and appreciate Clarify and support spoken messages using appropriate props such as objects, pictures, or charts Record knowledge of a topic in various ways, such as by drawing pictures, making lists, and showing connections among ideas Respond appropriately and courteously to directions and questions	Model, create, and describe division situations in which a set of concrete objects is separated into equivalent sets	Describe the requirements of various jobs and the characteristics of a job well-performed Express ideas orally based on knowledge and experiences Describe ways that families meet basic human needs Describe similarities and differences in ways families meet basic needs	Identify characteristics of living organisms Identify characteristics of living organisms that allow their basic needs to be met

Activity	TEKS: Language Arts and Reading	TEKS: Mathematics	TEKS: Social Studies	TEKS: Science
19	Discuss meanings of words and develop vocabulary through meaningful and concrete experiences Record knowledge of a topic in various ways, such as by drawing pictures, making lists, and showing connections among ideas Respond appropriately and courteously to directions and questions Determine the purposes for listening, such as to get information, to solve problems, and to enjoy and appreciate			Identify characteristics of living organisms Make decisions using information Construct reasonable explanations and draw conclusions using information and prior knowledge
20	Discuss meanings of words and develop vocabulary through meaningful and concrete experiences Determine the purposes for listening, such as to get information, to solve problems, and to enjoy and appreciate Participate in rhymes, songs, conversations, and discussions Use vocabulary to describe clearly ideas, feelings, and experiences	Recall and apply basic addition facts Identify the mathematics in everyday situations Read a thermometer to gather data	Identify historic figures such as Amelia Earhart and Robert Fulton who have exhibited a love of individualism and inventiveness Explain how science and technology have changed the ways in which people meet basic needs Express ideas orally based on knowledge and experiences Identify characteristics and qualities of careers in science Express ideas orally based on knowledge and experiences	Identify characteristics of living organisms Compare and give examples of the ways living organisms depend on each other and on their environments Construct reasonable explanations and draw conclusions using information and prior knowledge Collect information using tools including rulers, meter sticks, measuring cups, clocks, hand lenses, computers, thermometers, and balances

Activity	TEKS: Language Arts and Reading	TEKS: Mathematics	TEKS: Social Studies	TEKS: Science
21	Participate in rhymes, songs, conversations, and discussions Discuss meanings of words and develop vocabulary through meaningful and concrete experiences Determine the purposes for listening, such as to get information, to solve problems, and to enjoy and appreciate Use knowledge of word order (syntax) and context to support word identification and confirm word meaning Record knowledge of a topic in various ways, such as by drawing pictures, making lists, and showing connections among ideas		Identify characteristics and qualities of careers in science Express ideas orally based on knowledge and experiences	Construct reasonable explanations and draw conclusions using information and prior knowledge Make decisions using information Gather information using simple equipment and tools to extend the senses Observe and record changes in weather from day to day and over seasons

Activity	TEKS: Language Arts and Reading	TEKS: Mathematics	TEKS: Social Studies	TEKS: Science
22	Discuss meanings of words and develop vocabulary through meaningful and concrete experiences Determine the purposes for listening, such as to get information, to solve problems, and to enjoy and appreciate Participate in rhymes, songs, conversations, and discussions Use vocabulary to describe clearly ideas, feelings, and experiences Record knowledge of a topic in various ways, such as by drawing pictures, making lists, and showing connections among ideas	Use numbers to describe how many objects are in a set Count by ones to 100 Measure length, capacity, and weight using concrete models that approximate standard units Use a problem-solving model that incorporates understanding the problem, making a plan, carrying out the plan, and evaluating the solution for reasonableness	Identify characteristics and qualities of careers in science Express ideas orally based on knowledge and experiences	Describe and illustrate the water cycle Identify characteristics of nonliving objects Demonstrate a change in the motion of an object by giving the object a push or a pull Construct reasonable explanations and draw conclusions using information and prior knowledge Identify, predict, and test uses of heat to cause change such as melting and evaporation Plan and conduct simple descriptive investigations

Activity	TEKS: Language Arts and Reading	TEKS: Mathematics	TEKS: Social Studies	TEKS: Science
23	Discuss meanings of words and develop vocabulary through meaningful and concrete experiences Determine the purposes for listening, such as to get information, to solve problems, and to enjoy and appreciate Participate in rhymes, songs, conversations, and discussions Use vocabulary to describe clearly ideas, feelings, and experiences Respond appropriately and courteously to directions and questions Produce rhyming words and distinguish rhyming words from non-rhyming words Identify the musical elements of literary language such as rhymes, repeated sounds, or instances of onomatopoeia Record knowledge of a topic in various ways, such as by drawing pictures, making lists, and showing connections among ideas		Identify characteristics and qualities of careers in science Express ideas orally based on knowledge and experiences	Construct reasonable explanations and draw conclusions using information and prior knowledge Make decisions using information Identify characteristics of nonliving objects Observe and record changes in weather from day to day and over seasons

Activity	TEKS: Language Arts and Reading	TEKS: Mathematics	TEKS: Social Studies	TEKS: Science
24	Determine the purposes for listening, such as to get information, to solve problems, and to enjoy and appreciate Record knowledge of a topic in various ways, such as by drawing pictures, making lists, and showing connections among ideas		Identify characteristics and qualities of careers in science Express ideas orally based on knowledge and experiences	Construct reasonable explanations and draw conclusions using information and prior knowledge Observe and record changes in weather from day to day and over seasons
25	Determine the purposes for listening, such as to get information, to solve problems, and to enjoy and appreciate Participate in rhymes, songs, conversations, and discussions Use vocabulary to describe clearly ideas, feelings, and experiences Respond appropriately and courteously to directions and questions Record knowledge of a topic in various ways, such as by drawing pictures, making lists, and showing connections among ideas	Compare and order whole numbers up to 99 (less than, greater than, or equal to) using sets of concrete objects and pictorial models Use a problem-solving model that incorporates understanding the problem, making a plan, carrying out the plan, and evaluating the solution for reasonableness Select addition or subtraction and solve problems using two-digit numbers, whether or not regrouping is necessary	Identify characteristics and qualities of careers in science Express ideas orally based on knowledge and experiences	Construct reasonable explanations and draw conclusions using information and prior knowledge Make decisions using information Identify characteristics of nonliving objects

Activity	TEKS: Language Arts and Reading	TEKS: Mathematics	TEKS: Social Studies	TEKS: Science
26	Discuss meanings of words and develop vocabulary through meaningful and concrete experiences Participate in rhymes, songs, conversations, and discussions Determine the purposes for listening, such as to get information, to solve problems, and to enjoy and appreciate Record knowledge of a topic in various ways, such as by drawing pictures, making lists, and showing connections among ideas		Identify characteristics and qualities of careers in science Express ideas orally based on knowledge and experiences	Construct reasonable explanations and draw conclusions using information and prior knowledge Make decisions using information Identify characteristics of nonliving objects
27	Respond appropriately and courteously to directions and questions Use vocabulary to describe clearly ideas, feelings, and experiences Participate in rhymes, songs, conversations, and discussions Determine the purposes for listening, such as to get information, to solve problems, and to enjoy and appreciate Record knowledge of a topic in various ways, such as by drawing pictures, making lists, and showing connections among ideas Listen responsively to stories and other texts read aloud, including selections from classic and contemporary works		Identify characteristics and qualities of careers in science Express ideas orally based on knowledge and experiences	Construct reasonable explanations and draw conclusions using information and prior knowledge Make decisions using information Identify characteristics of nonliving objects

Activity	TEKS: Language Arts and Reading	TEKS: Mathematics	TEKS: Social Studies	TEKS: Science
28	Respond appropriately and courteously to directions and questions Use vocabulary to describe clearly ideas, feelings, and experiences Participate in rhymes, songs, conversations, and discussions Determine the purposes for listening, such as to get information, to solve problems, and to enjoy and appreciate Record knowledge of a topic in various ways, such as by drawing pictures, making lists, and showing connections among ideas Listen responsively to stories and other texts read aloud, including selections from classic and contemporary works		Identify characteristics and qualities of careers in science Express ideas orally based on knowledge and experiences Identify historic figures such as Amelia Earhart and Robert Fulton, who have exhibited a love of individualism and inventiveness	Construct reasonable explanations and draw conclusions using information and prior knowledge Make decisions using information Identify characteristics of nonliving objects Demonstrate a change in the motion of an object by giving the object a push or a pull

Activity	TEKS: Language Arts and Reading	TEKS: Mathematics	TEKS: Social Studies	TEKS: Science
29	Determine the purposes for listening, such as to get information, to solve problems, and to enjoy and appreciate Record knowledge of a topic in various ways, such as by drawing pictures, making lists, and showing connections among ideas Use vocabulary to describe clearly ideas, feelings, and experiences Respond appropriately and courteously to directions and questions Use more complex capitalization and punctuation with increasing accuracy, such as proper nouns, abbreviations, commas, apostrophes, and question marks	Use a problem-solving model that incorporates understanding the problem, making a plan, carrying out the plan, and evaluating the solution for reasonableness Measure length, capacity, and weight using concrete models that approximate standard units	Identify characteristics and qualities of careers in science Express ideas orally based on knowledge and experiences	Construct reasonable explanations and draw conclusions using information and prior knowledge Make decisions using information Identify characteristics of nonliving objects

Activity	TEKS: Language Arts and Reading	TEKS: Mathematics	TEKS: Social Studies	TEKS: Science
30	Discuss meanings of words and develop vocabulary through meaningful/concrete experiences Determine the purpose(s) for listening such as to get information, to solve problems, and to enjoy and appreciate Listen critically to interpret and evaluate Participate in rhymes, songs, conversations, and discussions Write to record ideas and reflections Record his/her own knowledge of a topic in various ways such as by drawing pictures, making lists, and showing connections among ideas	Name fractional parts of a whole object (not to exceed twelfths) when given concrete representation Identify attributes of any shape or solid Measure length, capacity, and weight using concrete models that approximate standard units Describe one object in relation to another using informal language such as over, under, above, and below	Identify characteristics and qualities of careers in science Express ideas orally based on knowledge and experiences Create visual and written materials to express ideas	Demonstrate safe practices during classroom and field investigations Ask questions about organisms, objects, and events Construct reasonable explanations and draw conclusions using information and prior knowledge Identify, predict, replicate, and create patterns including those seen in charts, graphs, and numbers

Activity	TEKS: Language Arts and Reading	TEKS: Mathematics	TEKS: Social Studies	TEKS: Science
31	Determine the purpose(s) for listening such as to get information, to solve problems, and to enjoy and appreciate Listen critically to interpret and evaluate Participate in rhymes, songs, conversations, and discussions Write to record ideas and reflections Record his/her own knowledge of a topic in various ways such as by drawing pictures, making lists, and showing connections among ideas Ask and answer relevant questions and make contributions in small or large group discussions	Name fractional parts of a whole object (not to exceed twelfths) when given concrete representation Identify attributes of any shape or solid Draw conclusions and answer questions based on picture graphs and bar-type graphs	Identify major landforms and bodies of water, including continents and oceans, on maps and globes Use symbols, find locations, and determine directions on maps and globes Express ideas orally based on knowledge and experiences Create visual and written materials to express ideas	Ask questions about organisms, objects, and events Construct reasonable explanations and draw conclusions using information and prior knowledge Make decisions using information

Activity	TEKS: Language Arts and Reading	TEKS: Mathematics	TEKS: Social Studies	TEKS: Science
32	Discuss meanings of words and develop vocabulary through meaningful/concrete experiences Determine the purpose(s) for listening such as to get information, to solve problems, and to enjoy and appreciate Use vocabulary to describe clearly ideas, feelings, and experiences Connect experiences and ideas with those of others through speaking and listening Ask and answer relevant questions and make contributions in small or large group discussions Record his/her own knowledge of a topic in various ways such as by drawing pictures, making lists, and showing connections among ideas	Name fractional parts of a whole object (not to exceed twelfths) when given concrete representation Measure length, capacity, and weight using concrete models that approximate standard units Explain and record observations using objects, words, pictures, numbers, and technology		Demonstrate safe practices during classroom and field investigations Plan and conduct simple descriptive investigations Construct reasonable explanations and draw conclusions using information and prior knowledge Make decisions using information Communicate explanations about investigations
33	Determine the purpose(s) for listening such as to get information, to solve problems, and to enjoy and appreciate Read to accomplish various purposes, both assigned and self-selected Ask and answer relevant questions and make contributions in small or large group discussions Discuss meanings of words and develop vocabulary through meaningful/concrete experiences		Identify characteristics and qualities of careers in science Express ideas orally based on knowledge and experiences Identify historic figures such as Amelia Earhart and Robert Fulton who have exhibited a love of individualism and inventiveness	

Activity	TEKS: Language Arts and Reading	TEKS: Mathematics	TEKS: Social Studies	TEKS: Science
34	Discuss meanings of words and develop vocabulary through meaningful/concrete experiences Determine the purpose(s) for listening such as to get information, to solve problems, and to enjoy and appreciate Ask and answer relevant questions and make contributions in small or large group discussions Use multiple sources, including print such as an encyclopedia, technology, and experts, to locate information that addresses questions Record his/her own knowledge of a topic in various ways such as by drawing pictures, making lists, and showing connections among ideas		Identify characteristics and qualities of careers in science Express ideas orally based on knowledge and experiences	Identify characteristics of living organisms Identify the external characteristics of different kinds of plants and animals that allow their needs to be met Compare and give examples of the ways living organisms depend on each other and on their environment Communicate explanations about investigations

Activity	TEKS: Language Arts and Reading	TEKS: Mathematics	TEKS: Social Studies	TEKS: Science
35	Discuss meanings of words and develop vocabulary through meaningful/concrete experiences Determine the purpose(s) for listening such as to get information, to solve problems, and to enjoy and appreciate Ask and answer relevant questions and make contributions in small or large group discussions Use vocabulary to describe clearly ideas, feelings, and experiences Connect experiences and ideas with those of others through speaking and listening Participate in rhymes, songs, conversations, and discussions Record his/her own knowledge of a topic in various ways such as by drawing pictures, making lists, and showing connections among ideas	Measure length, capacity, and weight using concrete models that approximate standard units Explain and record observations using objects, words, pictures, numbers, and technology Construct picture graphs and bar-type graphs Draw conclusions and answer questions based on picture graphs and bar-type graphs	Identify characteristics and qualities of careers in science Express ideas orally based on knowledge and experiences Create visual and written materials to express ideas	Identify characteristics of living organisms Identify the external characteristics of different kinds of plants and animals that allow their needs to be met Demonstrate safe practices during classroom and field investigations Ask questions about organisms, objects, and events Plan and conduct simple descriptive investigations Construct reasonable explanations and draw conclusions using information and prior knowledge

Activity	TEKS: Language Arts and Reading	TEKS: Mathematics	TEKS: Social Studies	TEKS: Science
36	Discuss meanings of words and develop vocabulary through meaningful/concrete experiences Determine the purpose(s) for listening such as to get information, to solve problems, and to enjoy and appreciate Ask and answer relevant questions and make contributions in small or large group discussions Use vocabulary to describe clearly ideas, feelings, and experiences Participate in rhymes, songs, conversations, and discussions Record his/her own knowledge of a topic in various ways such as by drawing pictures, making lists, and showing connections among ideas	Describe time on a clock using hours and minutes Use a problem-solving model that incorporates understanding the problem, making a plan, carrying out the plan, and evaluating the solution for reasonableness	Identify characteristics and qualities of careers in science Express ideas orally based on knowledge and experiences Create visual and written materials to express ideas	Identify characteristics of living organisms Identify the external characteristics of different kinds of plants and animals that allow their needs to be met Construct reasonable explanations and draw conclusions using information and prior knowledge

Activity	TEKS: Language Arts and Reading	TEKS: Mathematics	TEKS: Social Studies	TEKS: Science
37	Record his/her own knowledge of a topic in various ways such as by drawing pictures, making lists, and showing connections among ideas Write to record ideas and reflections Use vocabulary to describe clearly ideas, feelings, and experiences Discuss meanings of words and develop vocabulary through meaningful/concrete experiences		Identify characteristics and qualities of careers in science Express ideas orally based on knowledge and experiences Create visual and written materials to express ideas	Identify characteristics of living organisms Identify the external characteristics of different kinds of plants and animals that allow their needs to be met Compare and give examples of the ways living organisms depend on each other and on their environment Observe, measure, record, analyze, predict, and illustrate changes in size, mass, temperature, color, position, quantity, sound, and movement Communicate explanations about investigations
38	Participate in rhymes, songs, conversations, and discussions Write to record ideas and reflections Record his/her own knowledge of a topic in various ways such as by drawing pictures, making lists, and showing connections among ideas Use alphabetical order to locate information	Identify, extend, and create patterns of sounds, physical movement, and concrete objects Use patterns to predict what comes next, including cause-and-effect relationships Identify the mathematics in everyday situations Use a problem-solving model that incorporates understanding the problem, making a plan, carrying out the plan, and evaluating the solution for reasonableness		Identify characteristics of living organisms Make decisions using information

Activity	TEKS: Language Arts and Reading	TEKS: Mathematics	TEKS: Social Studies	TEKS: Science
39	Use multiple sources, including print such as an encyclopedia, technology, and experts to locate information that addresses questions Draw conclusions from information gathered Write to record ideas and reflections Record his/her own knowledge of a topic in various ways such as by drawing pictures, making lists, and showing connections among ideas Use vocabulary to describe clearly ideas, feelings, and experiences Discuss meanings of words and develop vocabulary through meaningful/concrete experiences		Identify characteristics and qualities of careers in science Express ideas orally based on knowledge and experiences Create visual and written materials to express ideas	Identify characteristics of living organisms Make decisions using information
40	Determine the purpose(s) for listening such as to get information, to solve problems, and to enjoy and appreciate Write to record ideas and reflections Record his/her own knowledge of a topic in various ways such as by drawing pictures, making lists, and showing connections among ideas Use vocabulary to describe clearly ideas, feelings, and experiences	Measure length, capacity, and weight using concrete models that approximate standard units Recall and apply basic addition facts Select addition or subtraction and solve problems using two-digit numbers, whether or not regrouping is necessary Use tools such as real objects, manipulatives, and technology to solve problems	Identify characteristics and qualities of careers in science Express ideas orally based on knowledge and experiences Create visual and written materials to express ideas Identify major landforms and bodies of water, including continents and oceans, on maps and globes	Identify characteristics of living organisms Construct reasonable explanations and draw conclusions using information and prior knowledge

Activity	TEKS: Language Arts and Reading	TEKS: Mathematics	TEKS: Social Studies	TEKS: Science
41	Discuss meanings of words and develop vocabulary through meaningful/concrete experiences Use vocabulary to describe clearly ideas, feelings, and experiences Respond appropriately and courteously to directions and questions Participate in rhymes, songs, conversations, and discussions Connect experiences and ideas with those of others through speaking and listening Write to record ideas and reflections Record his/her own knowledge of a topic in various ways such as by drawing pictures, making lists, and showing connections among ideas Determine the purpose(s) for listening such as to get information, to solve problems, and to enjoy and appreciate		Identify characteristics and qualities of careers in science Express ideas orally based on knowledge and experiences	Ask questions about organisms, objects, and events Gather information using simple equipment and tools to extend the senses Construct reasonable explanations and draw conclusions using information and prior knowledge

Activity	TEKS: Language Arts and Reading	TEKS: Mathematics	TEKS: Social Studies	TEKS: Science
42	Discuss meanings of words and develop vocabulary through meaningful/concrete experiences Respond appropriately and courteously to directions and questions Connect experiences and ideas with those of others through speaking and listening Determine the purpose(s) for listening such as to get information, to solve problems, and to enjoy and appreciate Draw conclusions from information gathered		Identify characteristics and qualities of careers in science Express ideas orally based on knowledge and experiences	Ask questions about organisms, objects, and events Plan and conduct simple descriptive investigations Gather information using simple equipment and tools to extend the senses Construct reasonable explanations and draw conclusions using information and prior knowledge Make decisions using information
43	Determine the purpose(s) for listening such as to get information, to solve problems, and to enjoy and appreciate Record his/her own knowledge of a topic in various ways such as by drawing pictures, making lists, and showing connections among ideas Use vocabulary to describe clearly ideas, feelings, and experiences Clarify and support spoken messages using appropriate props such as objects, pictures, or charts		Identify characteristics and qualities of careers in science Express ideas orally based on knowledge and experiences	Construct reasonable explanations and draw conclusions using information and prior knowledge Make decisions using information Discuss and justify the merits of decisions

Activity	TEKS: Language Arts and Reading	TEKS: Mathematics	TEKS: Social Studies	TEKS: Science
44	Discuss meanings of words and develop vocabulary through meaningful/concrete experiences Respond appropriately and courteously to directions and questions Connect experiences and ideas with those of others through speaking and listening Determine the purpose(s) for listening such as to get information, to solve problems, and to enjoy and appreciate Participate in rhymes, songs, conversations, and discussions Connect experiences and ideas with those of others through speaking and listening		Identify characteristics and qualities of careers in science Express ideas orally based on knowledge and experiences Obtain information about a topic using a variety of visual sources such as pictures, graphics, television, maps, computer software, literature, reference sources, and artifacts	Identify characteristics of living organisms Identify characteristics of nonliving objects Identify the external characteristics of different kinds of plants and animals that allow their needs to be met Compare and give examples of the ways living organisms depend on each other and on their environment Construct reasonable explanations and draw conclusions using information and prior knowledge Make decisions using information
45	Determine the purpose(s) for listening such as to get information, to solve problems, and to enjoy and appreciate Participate in rhymes, songs, conversations, and discussions Respond appropriately and courteously to directions and questions Connect experiences and ideas with those of others through speaking and listening		Identify characteristics and qualities of careers in science Express ideas orally based on knowledge and experiences Obtain information about a topic using a variety of visual sources such as pictures, graphics, television, maps, computer software, literature, reference sources, and artifacts Use symbols, find locations, and determine directions on maps and globes Locate the community, Texas, the United States, and selected countries on maps and globes	Construct reasonable explanations and draw conclusions using information and prior knowledge Make decisions using information Observe, measure, record, analyze, predict, and illustrate changes in size, mass, temperature, color, position, quantity, sound, and movement

Activity	TEKS: Language Arts and Reading	TEKS: Mathematics	TEKS: Social Studies	TEKS: Science
46	Discuss meanings of words and develop vocabulary through meaningful/concrete experiences Respond appropriately and courteously to directions and questions Connect experiences and ideas with those of others through speaking and listening Record his/her own knowledge of a topic in various ways such as by drawing pictures, making lists, and showing connections among ideas Write to record ideas and reflections Ask and answer relevant questions and make contributions in small or large group discussions Determine the purpose(s) for listening such as to get information, to solve problems, and to enjoy and appreciate		Identify characteristics and qualities of careers in science Express ideas orally based on knowledge and experiences	Construct reasonable explanations and draw conclusions using information and prior knowledge Make decisions using information Observe, measure, record, analyze, predict, and illustrate changes in size, mass temperature, color, position, quantity, sound, and movement Discuss and justify the merits of decisions Demonstrate a change in the motion of an object by giving the object a push or a pull

Activity	TEKS: Language Arts and Reading	TEKS: Mathematics	TEKS: Social Studies	TEKS: Science
47	Discuss meanings of words and develop vocabulary through meaningful/concrete experiences Respond appropriately and courteously to directions and questions Connect experiences and ideas with those of others through speaking and listening Ask and answer relevant questions and make contributions in small or large group discussions Determine the purpose(s) for listening such as to get information, to solve problems, and to enjoy and appreciate Record his/her own knowledge of a topic in various ways such as by drawing pictures, making lists, and showing connections among ideas	Select or develop an appropriate problem-solving model, with guidance as needed, that incorporates understanding the problem, making a plan, carrying out the plan, and evaluation the solution for reasonableness Explain and record observations using objects, words, pictures, numbers, and technology Construct picture graphs and bar-type graphs	Identify characteristics and qualities of careers in science Express ideas orally based on knowledge and experiences	Plan and conduct simple descriptive investigations Gather information using simple equipment and tools to extend the senses Construct reasonable explanations and draw conclusions using information and prior knowledge Make decisions using information Observe, measure, record, analyze, predict, and illustrate changes in size, mass temperature, color, position, quantity, sound, and movement Discuss and justify the merits of decisions Demonstrate a change in the motion of an object by giving the object a push or a pull

Activity	TEKS: Language Arts and Reading	TEKS: Mathematics	TEKS: Social Studies	TEKS: Science
48	Discuss meanings of words and develop vocabulary through meaningful/concrete experiences Respond appropriately and courteously to directions and questions Connect experiences and ideas with those of others through speaking and listening Record his/her own knowledge of a topic in various ways such as by drawing pictures, making lists, and showing connections among ideas Participate in rhymes, songs, conversations, and discussions	Measure length, capacity, and weight using concrete models that approximate standard units Explain and record observations using objects, words, pictures, numbers, and technology	Identify characteristics and qualities of careers in science Express ideas orally based on knowledge and experiences	Plan and conduct simple descriptive investigations Gather information using simple equipment and tools to extend the senses Construct reasonable explanations and draw conclusions using information and prior knowledge Make decisions using information Observe, measure, record, analyze, predict, and illustrate changes in size, mass temperature, color, position, quantity, sound, and movement

Activity	TEKS: Language Arts and Reading	TEKS: Mathematics	TEKS: Social Studies	TEKS: Science
49	Connect experiences and ideas with those of others through speaking and listening Record his/her own knowledge of a topic in various ways such as by drawing pictures, making lists, and showing connections among ideas Read to accomplish various purposes, both assigned and self-selected Discuss meanings of words and develop vocabulary through meaningful/concrete experiences Respond appropriately and courteously to directions and questions Determine the purpose(s) for listening such as to get information, to solve problems, and to enjoy and appreciate	Select addition or subtraction and solve problems using two-digit numbers, whether or not regrouping is necessary Identify the mathematics in everyday situations Select or develop an appropriate problem-solving model, with guidance as needed, that incorporates understanding the problem, making a plan, carrying out the plan, and evaluation the solution for reasonableness	Identify characteristics and qualities of careers in science Express ideas orally based on knowledge and experiences Identify historic figures such as Amelia Earhart and Robert Fulton who have exhibited a love of individualism and inventiveness	
50	Discuss meanings of words and develop vocabulary through meaningful/concrete experiences Respond appropriately and courteously to directions and questions Connect experiences and ideas with those of others through speaking and listening Ask and answer relevant questions and make contributions in small or large group discussions Participate in rhymes, songs, conversations, and discussions		Identify characteristics and qualities of careers in science Express ideas orally based on knowledge and experiences	Construct reasonable explanations and draw conclusions using information and prior knowledge Make decisions using information

Printed in the United States
by Baker & Taylor Publisher Services